CORAL
WONDERLAND

THE BEST DIVE SITES OF THE GREAT BARRIER REEF & CORAL SEA

Nigel Marsh

First published in 2016 by New Holland Publishers Pty Ltd
London • Sydney • Auckland

The Chandlery, Unit 704, 50 Westminster Bridge Road, London
SE1 7QY, United Kingdom
1/66 Gibbes Street, Chatswood, NSW 2067, Australia
5/39 Woodside Avenue, Northcote, Auckland 0627 New Zealand

www.newhollandpublishers.com

A record of this book is held at the British Library and the
National Library of Australia.

ISBN 9781921517808

Managing Director: Fiona Schultz
Publisher: Diane Ward
Project Editor: Holly Willsher
Designer: Andrew Davies
Maps: Andrew Davies
Production Director: James Mills-Hicks
Printer: Toppan Leefung Printing Limited
10 9 8 7 6 5 4 3 2 1

Keep up with New Holland Publishers on Facebook
www.facebook.com/NewHollandPublishers

To Jack and Jean Marsh, my wonderful supportive parents who are greatly missed.

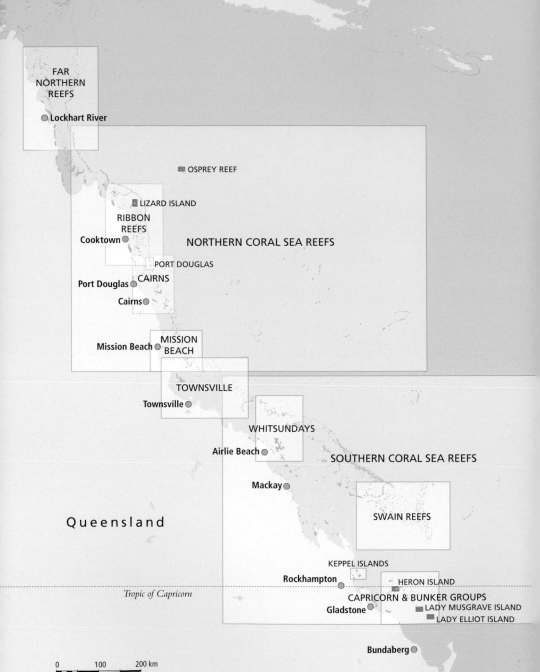

Papua
New
Guinea

Port Moresby

FAR
NORTHERN
REEFS

Lockhart River

OSPREY REEF

LIZARD ISLAND

RIBBON
REEFS

NORTHERN CORAL SEA REEFS

Cooktown

PORT DOUGLAS

CAIRNS

Port Douglas

Cairns

MISSION
BEACH

Mission Beach

TOWNSVILLE

Townsville

WHITSUNDAYS

SOUTHERN CORAL SEA REEFS

Airlie Beach

Mackay

Queensland

SWAIN REEFS

KEPPEL ISLANDS

Rockhampton

HERON ISLAND

Tropic of Capricorn

CAPRICORN & BUNKER GROUPS

Gladstone

LADY MUSGRAVE ISLAND

LADY ELLIOT ISLAND

Bundaberg

| 0 | 100 | 200 km |
| 0 | 50 | 100 n mile |

CONTENTS

OPPOSITE: A guide to the maps featured in this book.

OPPOSITE: A diver explores a colourful wall of coral on the Great Barrier Reef.

ACKNOWLEDGEMENTS

The author has spent almost forty years exploring the waters of the Great Barrier Reef and would like to thank the following people and dive operators for support in diving this area and making this book possible. Mike Ball (Mike Ball Dive Expeditions), Trina Baker (Spirit of Freedom & Tusa Dive), James McVeigh (Big Cat Reality), Megan Bell (Quicksilver Group), Greg Laurent (Kiana Charters), Ruth Appleyard (Heron Island Resort), Vicki Mullins (Lady Elliot Eco Resort), Lady Musgrave Charters, Julian Negri (Bundaberg Aqua Scuba), Fozzy (Mission Beach Dive), John Gransbury, Jerry Comans, Wayne Ingliss, Denis Kemp and John McGregor. I would also like to thank my cousin Jack Marsh, for first introducing me to the Great Barrier Reef and my dear late friend Neville Coleman, for being such a wonderful inspiration. To all those fabulous dive buddies (far too many to mention) that I have explored this amazing area with, thankyou for putting up with me as I snap countless images. And finally I would like to thank my number one dive buddy, my wonderful wife Helen Rose.

OPPOSITE: Giant soldierfish are a common species on the Great Barrier Reef and usually found sheltering in caves.

OVERLEAF: Beautiful coral gardens are a feature of the Great Barrier Reef and play host to many colourful fish species.

INTRODUCTION

The Great Barrier Reef is recognised as one of the seven wonders of the natural world and also as one of the best places to dive on the planet. Stretching over 2300km and comprising of over 3000 individual reefs, the Great Barrier Reef is immense, the world's largest reef system. Covering such a large area many first time visitors ask the question – 'where is the best place to dive on the Great Barrier Reef?'

The simple answer is there is no one place where you can see it all, as the Great Barrier Reef varies greatly across its entire range. Over 1500 fish species have been recorded on the Great Barrier Reef, however divers see different fish species in the north compared to the south. Also different areas of the Great Barrier Reef have very different attractions, like the manta rays of Lady Elliot Island or the potato cod of the Ribbon Reefs.

While there are many different destinations on the Great Barrier Reef there are also many different ways to visit this coral wonderland – from day boats, liveaboard dive boats and you can even stay on the reef at one of the many island resorts. The choices are endless; it will all depend on how much time you have and what you want to see.

To make those choices a little easier this guide book details all the main dive destinations and the best dive sites across the entire Great Barrier Reef, and even goes beyond to explore the legendary Coral Sea Reefs. Information is also provided on the best time to visit each area, typical conditions and a list of dive operators.

Finally, the Great Barrier Reef is alive and well (at the time of writing) and far from dead as reported by some in the media. The Great Barrier Reef is a living thing, ever changing and quick to recover from damage caused by cyclones. However, the Great Barrier Reef, and all coral reefs around the world, face numerous threats from climate change, warming seas, coral bleaching, agricultural runoff and crown-of-thorns starfish infestations.

The best way for people to protect the Great Barrier Reef, and ensure its future, is to visit this divers paradise. Tourists visiting the Great Barrier Reef inject over five billion dollars into the Australian economy each year, enough money that it keeps pressure on the Australian Government to ensure it is doing the right thing to protect this coral wonderland for future generations to enjoy.

ABOVE: Schools of painted sweetlips and spangled emperor's are often seen around the wreck of the *Severance*, Lady Elliot Island.

DIVING THE GREAT BARRIER REEF

There are many different ways to dive the Great Barrier Reef. You can explore this immense area on day boats, liveaboards or from a dive resort, it will all depend on your experience, how much time you have, where you want to dive, how you want to dive and what you want to see.

DAY BOATS

Most people visit the Great Barrier Reef on a day boat, and for many people one day on the reef is good enough, they have visited one of the natural wonders of the world and can tick that off the bucket list. Day boats generally operate from the mainland, and as the Great Barrier Reef is generally 20km to 50km offshore these trips last all day. Some of these boats only take certified divers, but the great majority take a combination of divers and snorkelers.

When looking for a day boat first check how many dives they allow, most only head out for a double dive, but others schedule three dives in a trip, which can be better value. Also confirm what dive sites are visited, this is always weather depended, but they should be able to tell you if the boat visits inner reefs or outer reefs (which generally have the best visibility). Other boats may only visit inshore islands, which is often the case in the Whitsundays.

Day boats will generally provide dive gear as part of the ticket price (as well as lunch), but always confirm this, and if you have your own dive gear check if you can get a discount for using it. A final item to check before you book your day trip is dive time, what bottom times do they allow? With some boats on a tight schedule they limit bottom time to 40 minutes or less. For a new diver this may not be a problem, but for more experienced divers this can severely limited your diving. Shop around, as you will find that many of the boats allow enough time in the day for you to do 60 minute dives.

Day boats vary greatly in size and the number of divers they carry. It may seem that smaller boats would offer a more personalised service, but it all depends on staff numbers. A boat that takes out 20 people with 5 staff is not going to give the same service as a boat that takes out 50 people with 20 staff. Many experienced divers avoid the larger day boats that take up to 80 people. Now this may seem like cattle-truck diving, but these larger boats are so roomy that they rarely feel crowded. On most trips the larger boats generally have less than a dozen certified divers, the great majority of people being snorkelers or people doing a discover scuba experience. So don't choose a smaller boat over a larger boat thinking that you will be sharing the water with fewer divers, as this may not be the case.

Most day boats, large or small, offer obligatory dive guides, which can be good or bad depending on the quality of the guide. The good guides, which are fortunately most of them, take their time, point out interesting species and allow people time to take photos and explore. The bad ones race through a dive like they have better things to do back on the boat and don't have time to show you anything. It is generally easy to tell the difference between the two. The good guides have been diving for a long time, love all marine life and are very keen to share the wonders of the Great Barrier Reef with every diver they meet. The bad guides are the ones that see diving as a job and nothing more, they usually know nothing about the creatures of the reef and don't seem to care about them either. A quick chat with your guide, prior to the dive, will often tell you what type of diver they are.

If you hate diving with a guide check with the boat before you book as quite a few allow experienced buddy teams to do their own thing. This is preferable for underwater photographers who like to take their dives slow while looking for subjects.

Day boats are perfect if you only have one or two days available to explore the Great Barrier Reef. But if you have longer then you should consider either a liveaboard boat or a stay at an island dive resort.

DIVE RESORTS

While there are hundreds of resorts and hotels on the mainland adjacent to the Great Barrier Reef, the number of resorts on islands located within reef waters is very limited. But staying on one of these islands is a fabulous way to explore the reef.

OPPOSITE: Green turtles are a common species on the Great Barrier Reef as they feed, breed and nest in reef waters.

OVERLEAF: Giant clams were once poached in alarming numbers by illegal Asian fishers, but their numbers have rebounded and these massive molluscs are now seen at dive sites across the Great Barrier Reef.

Resorts are found on Lizard Island, Fitzroy Island, Magnetic Island, the Whitsundays and Great Keppel Island. All these islands are continental islands, and have good diving around them on pretty coral gardens. However, if you want to dive the reef you will still have to board a day boat, but fortunately it will be a shorter day with less travel time. Resorts on coral cays like Heron Island and Lady Elliot Island are situated on the reef and are the main location you will be diving, meaning less travel time and more time spent underwater.

Thirty years ago there was once a floating hotel on a reef off Townsville, designed so people could stay overnight on the reef. The hotel never lived up to expectations and after only a few years it was shipped off to Vietnam. But for those that want to sleep overnight on the reef, and don't like rocking boats, that option is still available. Reefsleep is a pontoon off the Whitsundays where guests can sleep and then dive or snorkel the local reefs. The pontoon has cabins, or guests can sleep out under the stars. Of course the best way to sleep and dive on the reef is via a liveaboard boat.

LIVEABOARD BOATS

If you are an experienced diver, or if you just want to see the best areas of the Great Barrier Reef, then a liveaboard boat is the only way to go. Liveaboard boats operate to almost every area of the reef, including areas visited by day boats. But these vessels also visit remote areas of the Great Barrier Reef and the Coral Sea Reefs, which are way beyond the reach of day boats.

Liveaboard trips on the Great Barrier Reef vary in length from two days to ten days, but most of the popular trips are generally four to seven days long. The big advantage of a liveaboard trip is being able to do unlimited diving, usually four to six dives a day. And when you factor in saving on accommodation and meals, liveaboard diving can often work out cheaper per dive than staying at a resort and doing day trips.

Experienced divers enjoy liveaboard diving for the freedom it provides. Guides are available on these trips if required, but generally you and your dive buddy are free to do your own thing. Another advantage is being able to night dive on the reef and see all the amazing creatures that emerge after dark, something that day boats rarely do.

Of course not all liveaboards are the same, which is reflected in the price you pay for the trip. The top end liveaboards have roomy cabins with their own ensuite, while cheaper ones have share cabins and bathrooms. The cost difference will also be reflected in meals, crew numbers, boat comfort and even where you dive. But even the most basic liveaboard boat can be a great experience and take you to some incredible dive sites in this coral wonderland.

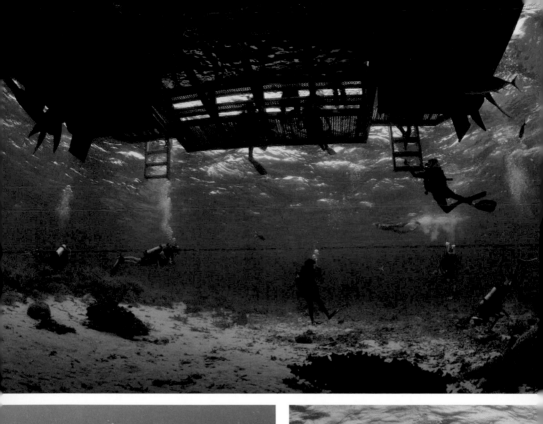

DIVER TRAINING

The Great Barrier Reef is the perfect place to do your first dive or even to complete a dive course. Dive shops are located in all the major towns adjacent to the reef and on resort islands, and are ready to teach you to scuba dive.

If you don't want to do a full scuba course, then a discover scuba experience is the way to go. These are available on most of the day boats and many of the resorts. A discover scuba experience will involve some basic instruction and then a shallow water dive with an instructor. It's a great introduction to the underwater world of the Great Barrier Reef, and some people are happy to try it once, but quite a few people then go on to do a full scuba course.

A full scuba course, to certify you as an open water diver, will generally take four days to complete, and will include classroom sessions, pool dives and open ocean dives. The main training agencies in Australia are PADI, SSI and NAUI, which are recognised around the world. Before you do a dive course you will have to pass a dive medical to show you are fit to dive (in accordance with Australian Standard AS4005.1). Once qualified as an open water diver you can dive to 18m anywhere in the world, but to dive deeper you will need to do an advanced course.

Becoming certified as an open water diver will open up a whole new world, but it is only the first step in your diver education as there are many speciality courses that can also be completed, such as nitrox diver, deep diver, wreck diver, night diver or rescue diver.

DIVING RULES AND REGULATIONS

Considering that millions of dives are completed on the Great Barrier Reef every year there are very few diving accidents or deaths. This is because diving is generally quite a safe sport and in Queensland there are very strict rules and regulations that all dive operators must follow to ensure diver safety.

All divers wishing to explore the waters of the Great Barrier Reef must be certified and must be able to produce a recognised certification card (c-card). If you don't have a c-card or can't provide proof that you are certified you may not be allowed to dive. Also all divers must carry a snorkel, whistle and

OPPOSITE, CLOCKWISE FROM TOP: Divers linger under a large dive boat in the clear water at Agincourt Reef, Port Douglas; exploring the rich coral gardens anywhere on the Great Barrier Reef is an experience that all divers will enjoy; potato cod are seen at many sites on the Great Barrier Reef, but for a very close encounter with these giant gropers divers need to explore the legendary Cod Hole on the Ribbon Reefs.

surface marker (safety sausage) on every dive. Currents are common on the Great Barrier Reef, which can lead to divers getting separated or lost. Having a surface maker will ensure that you are easier to locate on the surface, especially in choppy seas.

In Queensland all divers must dive with a buddy. If you don't have a buddy you will be paired up with someone of equal experience. But a few dive operators allow suitably qualified divers, with a backup air supply, to do solo diving.

All the dive boats operating on the Great Barrier Reef have to meet strict survey requirements and carry standard safety equipment (radio, oxygen, first aid, etc.) and the crew are trained to use it. They also have to fill out a logbook and follow standard safety procedures. All divers are recorded on a log, and after every dive the diver's details are recorded (depth and bottom time), and before the boat can move the log has to be signed off by the diver.

While divers are in the water a safety lookout is on watch at all times, making sure that no diver (or snorkeler) is in trouble at the surface. Tender boats are kept at standby at all times to quickly pickup any diver (or snorkeler) in trouble. Finally, head counts are done after each dive and before a boat moves to ensure that everyone is safely on board.

The diving rules and regulations in Queensland may seem a bit draconian at times, but they are in place to ensure that you have the safest diving experience possible while exploring the Great Barrier Reef.

DIVING ACCIDENTS

Considering how many people dive on the Great Barrier Reef each year, very few diving related accidents or deaths occur. In the case of a diving emergency every dive charter boat operating in reef waters carries first aid and oxygen, and all crew are training in its use. The crew will also contact the Diving Emergency Service (DES) to coordinate treatment and evacuation if required.

Queensland has a good network of hospitals that can deal with any medical emergency. However, there are only two recompression (hyperbaric) chambers in the state, located in Townsville and Brisbane for the treatment of decompression sickness (the bends) and other diving related illnesses. Fortunately they see very few cases of the bends, and the chambers are mainly used for other medical procedures.

OPPOSITE: An encounter you will never forget is watching the graceful dance of a manta ray. While manta rays are seen at many locations on the Great Barrier Reef, Lady Elliot Island is recognised as a manta hot spot.

Everyone travelling to Australia to dive should have travel insurance and dive insurance, to cover you in the case of a diving emergency. Divers Alert Network (DAN) Asia Pacific provides a comprehensive dive insurance plan in Australia (visit their website www.danap.org), but divers from overseas will find similar organisations in their own country. A policy costs less than one hundred dollars per year, but it could not only save your life, but save you thousands of dollars if you have to be evacuated.

In a diving emergency, or if you have symptoms that concern you after diving, such as joint soreness or rashes, contact DES for assistance and advice on 1800 088 200.

DIVING CONDITIONS

The Great Barrier Reef can be dived year round, with no real good season or bad season to factor into your planning. But with the Great Barrier Reef covering such a vast stretch of ocean, and being such a long way offshore, divers have to be prepared for choppy seas and windy conditions at any time.

Many people consider winter time (May to August) the best time to dive the Great Barrier Reef. The weather at this time of year is more stable but quite windy, with the southeast trade winds blowing 15 to 30 knots. In general the best time to visit the Great Barrier Reef is spring to early summer (September to December), as at this time of year the winds drop and seas calm. December and January can be a time of doldrums, with no wind and glassy seas. While the wet season (February to April) sees regular afternoon thunderstorms and changeable winds. But with the weather very unpredictable you shouldn't take any of this as gospel, as the reef can have calm conditions just as easy as rough conditions at any time of the year.

Cyclone season in Queensland is from November to April, with around five cyclones each year passing through the area, mostly in the north. Cyclones can impact on diving, causing rough seas and very strong winds, but if they pass quickly they may have no effect on the diving or delay diving for only a day or two. However, major cyclones have hit the coast and cause damage to boats and property, and interrupt diving for up to a week. Fortunately these events are rare. One thing you must realise is that cyclones are usually a local event, and with the Great Barrier Reef over 2300km long a cyclone can be hitting north of Cairns,

OPPOSITE: Broadclub cuttlefish are often encountered at dive sites on the Ribbon Reefs and Agincourt Reefs.

while everything south of Townsville can be calm and unaffected. Some people avoid diving the reef during cyclone season, but in reality little diving is missed each year due to cyclones.

Most boats generally don't cancel dives unless conditions are too rough to safely journey to the reef, this would be a combination of a large swell (over 2m seas) and strong winds (over 30 knots). The large catamaran dive boats used on the reef can handle some pretty rough conditions, cutting through the swell with ease. The roughest period of a dive trip is generally the crossing to the reef and back to the mainland, as once tucked up behind a reef it provides shelter and surprisingly calm conditions. If you get seasick, you are highly recommended to take seasickness prevention medication while diving the Great Barrier Reef.

The water temperature on the Great Barrier Reef varies greatly depending on the season and where you dive. In the north the water temperature varies from summer highs of 29°C to winter lows of 24°C. While in the south, 2000km away, the water temperature varies from summer highs of 27°C to winter lows of a chilly 19°C. In summer most divers use a 3mm wetsuit, while in winter 5mm wetsuits are popular.

The water clarity on the Great Barrier Reef is generally excellent, 15m to 30m on average. But outer reefs always have clearer water than inner reefs. Visibility around the continental islands within reef waters is usually in the range of 5m to 15m. The best visibility in this area is found on the remote Coral Sea Reefs, which usually have 30m to 45m visibility, but can be over 60m at times.

OPPOSITE: Many beautiful fish can be observed on the Great Barrier Reef, including the beaked coralfish.

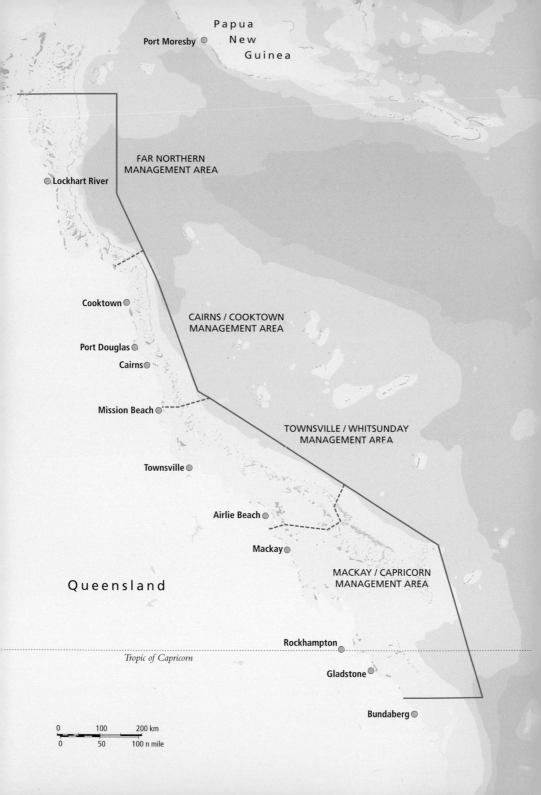

Papua
New
Guinea

Port Moresby ⊙

FAR NORTHERN
MANAGEMENT AREA

⊙ Lockhart River

Cooktown ⊙

CAIRNS / COOKTOWN
MANAGEMENT AREA

Port Douglas ⊙

Cairns ⊙

Mission Beach ⊙

TOWNSVILLE / WHITSUNDAY
MANAGEMENT AREA

Townsville ⊙

Airlie Beach ⊙

Mackay ⊙

Queensland

MACKAY / CAPRICORN
MANAGEMENT AREA

Rockhampton ⊙

Tropic of Capricorn

Gladstone ⊙

Bundaberg ⊙

0   100   200 km

0   50   100 n mile

GREAT BARRIER REEF MARINE PARK

In 1975 the Great Barrier Reef became the world's largest marine park, and the Great Barrier Reef Marine Park Authority (GBRMPA) was formed to manage this immense area. The marine park now covers an area of 345,000 square kilometres and has different zones to allow multiple users access to the reef. But getting the reef protected proved to be a real battle for conservationists.

HISTORY

The Great Barrier Reef we see today is thought to be around 8000 years old, formed after the last great ice age, and has been exploited for its natural resources since Europeans settled in Australia. While Aboriginals and Torres Strait Islanders have fished and hunted these waters for thousands of years, they had little impact compared to the European settlers who took sea cucumbers, turtles, dugongs and fish in alarming numbers.

Some forward thinking saw parts of the Great Barrier Reef declared as national parks, like Green Island in 1936 and Heron Island in 1943, before these areas could be ruined. However, the great majority of the reef was seen as a natural resource that could be used and exploited for tourism, fishing, shell collecting, coral collection and even mining.

In wasn't until the 1960s that conservation groups became concerned about the health and future of the Great Barrier Reef, starting the fight to get this natural wonder protected. At the forefront of this fight for the reef were the Wildlife Preservation Society of Queensland, the Australian Conservation Foundation and the Australian Marine Conservation Society (then known as

OPPOSITE: The Great Barrier Reef Marine Park covers such a large area that it has been spilt into four management zones (Map courtesy of the Spatial Data Centre, Great Barrier Reef Marine Park Authority 2016).

the Littoral Society of Queensland). But they were in for a tough battle as the Queensland Government at the time, which was charged with looking after the Great Barrier Reef, was only interested in growth, development and progress. Protecting the environment was at the bottom of their list of priorities.

The first battle started small, when Ellison Reef off Innisfail was under threat from proposed limestone mining in 1967. A company wanted to remove coral from this reef, which would have destroyed the reef and smothered adjacent reefs in silt. After an inquiry and objections from conservation groups the mining application was wisely denied.

But not long after this a bigger threat to the Great Barrier Reef emerged with the Queensland Government bestowing oil drilling permits to petroleum companies to drill in reef waters. The potential damage from an oil spill in reef waters could have been catastrophic, not to mention the damage from the drilling. Conservation groups were in for a long tough fight on this issue, but found this wasn't the only threat to the reef.

At the same time a massive outbreak of crown-of-thorns starfish was devastating the reef, and the Queensland Government was doing nothing to address the problem. The reef was also under attack from illegal fishers from Asia taking giant clams and other marine life in alarming numbers.

Conservation groups made numerous approaches to the Australian Commonwealth Government about the state of the reef, but they saw it as a Queensland Government issue, so didn't want to get involved. But the conservation groups never lost heart and managed to get people power behind them, with protest marches and other campaigns. With the tourism industry, fishing groups, the unions and the general public also calling for the Great Barrier Reef to be saved the Queensland and Commonwealth Governments finally had to sit up and take notice, and in 1970 a royal commission was called.

The Royal Commission into Exploratory and Production Drilling for Petroleum in the area of the Great Barrier Reef took four years to complete its hearings, but in the end it found that drilling for oil posed a serious threat to the Great Barrier Reef. The conservation groups and common sense had finally prevailed, both the Queensland Government and Commonwealth Government passed acts prohibiting petroleum drilling on the reef.

In 1975 the Commonwealth Government finally took control of the Great Barrier Reef away from the Queensland Government, passing the *Great*

OPPOSITE TOP: While exploring the Great Barrier Reef divers will see a wide variety of coral and fish species.

OPPOSITE BOTTOM: The pretty pink anemonefish lives in a symbiotic relationship with sea anemone. Both species benefit from this relationship, with the fish getting food and protection from predators, while protecting the sea anemone from its own predators.

Schools of diagonal-banded sweetlips are more commonly seen in northern reef water, especially on the Ribbon Reefs.

Barrier Reef Marine Park Act and establishing GBRMPA to manage this coral wonderland. But the Great Barrier Reef is not just a unique part of Australia, it is a very unique part of the planet, which was recognised when the reef was listed as a world heritage site in 1981.

GBRMPA today works hand in hand with the Queensland and Commonwealth Governments to manage, police, patrol and protect the Great Barrier Reef. One of their keys to success in managing the marine park was implementing a zoning system, which has since been employed by other marine parks around the world.

ZONINGS

While many think the Great Barrier Reef is protected as a giant marine sanctuary, the park is actually managed to allow multiple use by divers, fishers, tourism operators and others. To achieve this, different zonings are in place, which vary from the General Use Zone, where all activities are allowed to the Preservation Zone, where people are not allowed to enter without a permit.

Eight zones are in place across the reef, with diving allowed in all zones apart from the Preservation Zone. The most important area is the Marine National Park Zone or Green Zone, where no fishing of any kind is allowed. This zone makes up 33% of the marine park, but was originally only 5% when the park was first established, expanded in 2004 after a review. The Buffer Zone, making up 3% of the park, is similar but allows limited fishing. The same applies to the Habitat Protection Zone (28%) and Conservation Park Zone (2%). The Scientific Research Zone is an area set aside for research, but only accounts for 1% of the reef. While the Commonwealth Islands Zone (only 1%) encompasses and protects the islands in the Great Barrier Reef Area. The large General Use Zone (34%) is an area where both recreational and commercial fishing is allowed, but other activities like aquaculture and aquarium collecting are only allowed with a permit.

This zoning system doesn't please everyone, with fishers wanting access to Green Zones, and conservationists wanting more Green Zones, but it does achieve a balance that will hopefully see the Great Barrier Reef persevered for future generations to enjoy. (For more details about GBRMPA visit www.gbrmpa.gov.au)

CORAL SEA MARINE PARK

In November 2012 conservationists celebrated when the Coral Sea Reefs were finally protected, with the creation of the Coral Sea Commonwealth Marine Reserve. Covering an area of 989,842 square kilometres, the marine park is three times the size of the Great Barrier Reef Marine Park, and combined are the largest marine reserves in the world.

The remote reefs of the Coral Sea are very unique and very different to the reefs of the Great Barrier Reef. This immense area is also an important breeding and nesting area for turtles and sea birds, and a very special habitat for many pelagic fish, billfish, sharks, whales, dolphins and many other species.

The Coral Sea Marine Park has similar zonings to the Great Barrier Reef Marine Park, with 51% fully protected as Marine National Park Zone, 27% as Habitat Protection Zone, 2% as Conservation Park Zone and 20% open to General Use Zone.

But not long after the marine park was declared a new Commonwealth Government came into power and suspended all new commonwealth marine parks pending a review. This decision was very difficult to understand, as the marine park had been under review for 10 years, was based on sound scientific research and had the support of 95% of people and interested parties (750,000 submissions) that offered suggestions on the Coral Sea Marine Park.

OVERLEAF: Beautiful and delicate gorgonian fans decorate the walls and caves of the Great Barrier Reef.

THREATS TO THE GREAT BARRIER REEF

The Great Barrier Reef, like all reefs around the globe, faces a growing number of threats that may see this natural wonder of the world disappear, destroyed or diminished in the coming years.

CLIMATE CHANGE

The biggest threat to the future of the Great Barrier Reef is also the biggest threat to all ecosystems on the planet – climate change. Rising temperatures will have a devastating impact on coral reef communities, with increasing sea temperatures leading to more coral bleaching.

Coral bleaching occurs when water temperatures are higher than the corals can tolerate. This causes algae, that live in a complex symbiotic relationship inside the coral tissues and provide them with food, to die, leaving the coral white and dead. A number of coral bleaching events have already occurred on the Great Barrier Reef (in 1998 and 2002) and these events will become far more common unless climate change can be addressed.

Warming sea temperatures will also impact on many fish, marine reptiles and invertebrate species. While some species will be able to migrate to cooler waters, others will simply perish, from the destruction of their habitat and food sources. It is also unclear what impact warmer seas will have on the breeding cycle of corals, fish and many other species.

OPPOSITE LEFT: Hard corals are easily broken by careless divers or by boat anchors. All users of the reef should endeavour to minimise their impact on this fragile environment.

OPPOSITE RIGHT: Common coral trout are heavily targeted by fishers on the reef. On reefs that are fished they are rare, while on protected reefs in green zones they are a common species.

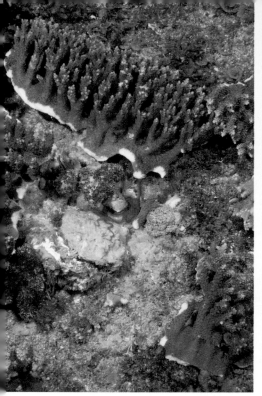

Other impacts associated with climate change are more frequent and more severe weather events, such as cyclones and flooding rains, rising sea levels and also ocean acidification. The threat of the ocean becoming more acidic may be a bigger problem than coral bleaching, which is often a localised event. This is caused by increasing levels of carbon dioxide in the atmosphere being absorbed by the oceans, then bonding with seawater to form carbonic acid, thus increasing the acidic levels. The fallout from this chemical reaction is less calcium carbonate in the water, which is a crucial ingredient used by corals, molluscs and crustaceans to build their skeletons. The impact of ocean acidification is still being studied and debated, but it will have a major impact on the marine environment unless carbon dioxide levels (the burning of fossil fuels) can be reduced.

WATER QUALITY

Over the last 150 years the population in Queensland has grown to over 4.7 million people. Along with this growth has been the development of land for agriculture, tourism, industry and residential housing, resulting in the destruction of forests and mangroves. The impact of this development has led to a decrease in water quality in rivers and the adjacent ocean, which has had a major effect on the Great Barrier Reef. This is from sediment, nutrients and pesticides being washed off the land and into rivers, and finally ending up on the reef. The Great Barrier Reef receives run-off from 35 major catchment areas in Queensland that cover an area of 424,000 square kilometres.

While much has been done to manage this run-off, it is difficult to control, especially in the wet season when flooding rains sweep across the land. Many inshore reefs are now dead, the corals smothered from sediment runoff. But more nutrients in the water causes other problems, like promoting the growth of algae, that can also smother corals and increases crown-of-thorns starfish populations.

Dredging has also impacted the water quality, with the dredging of river and harbours adding to inflated silt levels in the water. Dredging and the dumping of dredge spoil in reef waters has been a controversial issue over the last few years, due to the expansion and building of new port facilities along the Queensland coast for the export of coal. The backlash against these developments has been overwhelming, harking back to the days when the Queensland Government was allowing oil companies to explore and drill in reef waters. Common sense finally prevailed, with the Australian Government banning the disposal of capital dredge spoil in the marine park. However, these port expansions are still on the cards and will still require dredging. And if they proceed, this will also see an increase of ship movements in reef waters, which would be disastrous if one of these ships were to run aground.

CROWN-OF-THORNS

Crown-of-thorns starfish (COT) naturally occur in reef waters and pose no threat to coral unless their populations explode, which seems to happen every few years. Normally COT are part of a healthy coral reef ecosystem, feeding on the fast growing hard corals, thus allowing the slower growing corals a chance to establish. But when their populations swell they eat all the hard corals on a reef, which then allows algae to take over and leave the once colourful reef almost devoid of life. Fortunately the hard corals do come back, but it can take many years for a reef to recover from a major attack of COT.

COT outbreaks occur about every 17 years, and there have been four major outbreaks documented since the 1960s on the Great Barrier Reef. Each outbreak can last for years, and generally starts in the north and spreads south. Why the outbreaks occur is still not fully understood, but it is thought to be associated with increased nutrient levels in the water (from agricultural run-off) allowing for favourable conditions for the young COT to develop. But a reduction in the number of animals that prey on the COT, such as triton shells and Maori wrasse, may also be a factor.

An eradication and monitoring program is in place to control COT, with divers injecting the starfish with a sodium bisulphate solution to kill them. But with millions of COT it is a massive undertaking, and in many cases the COT eat themselves to death, by consuming all the corals on a reef, before they can be exterminated. Research is ongoing into the COT issue on the Great Barrier Reef.

We can only hope in years to come that threats to the Great Barrier Reef can be addressed and resolved, or future generations may not get a chance to enjoy this coral wonderland.

ABOVE LEFT: Moorings are typically used by dive boats throughout the Great Barrier Reef to avoid anchor damage to corals.

ABOVE RIGHT: Crown-of-thorns starfish are a naturally occurring species on the Great Barrier Reef, but can devastated corals when their numbers grow to plague proportions.

OVERLEAF: Divers will find spectacular coral gardens which exploring the reefs off Port Douglas.

THE DIVE SITES

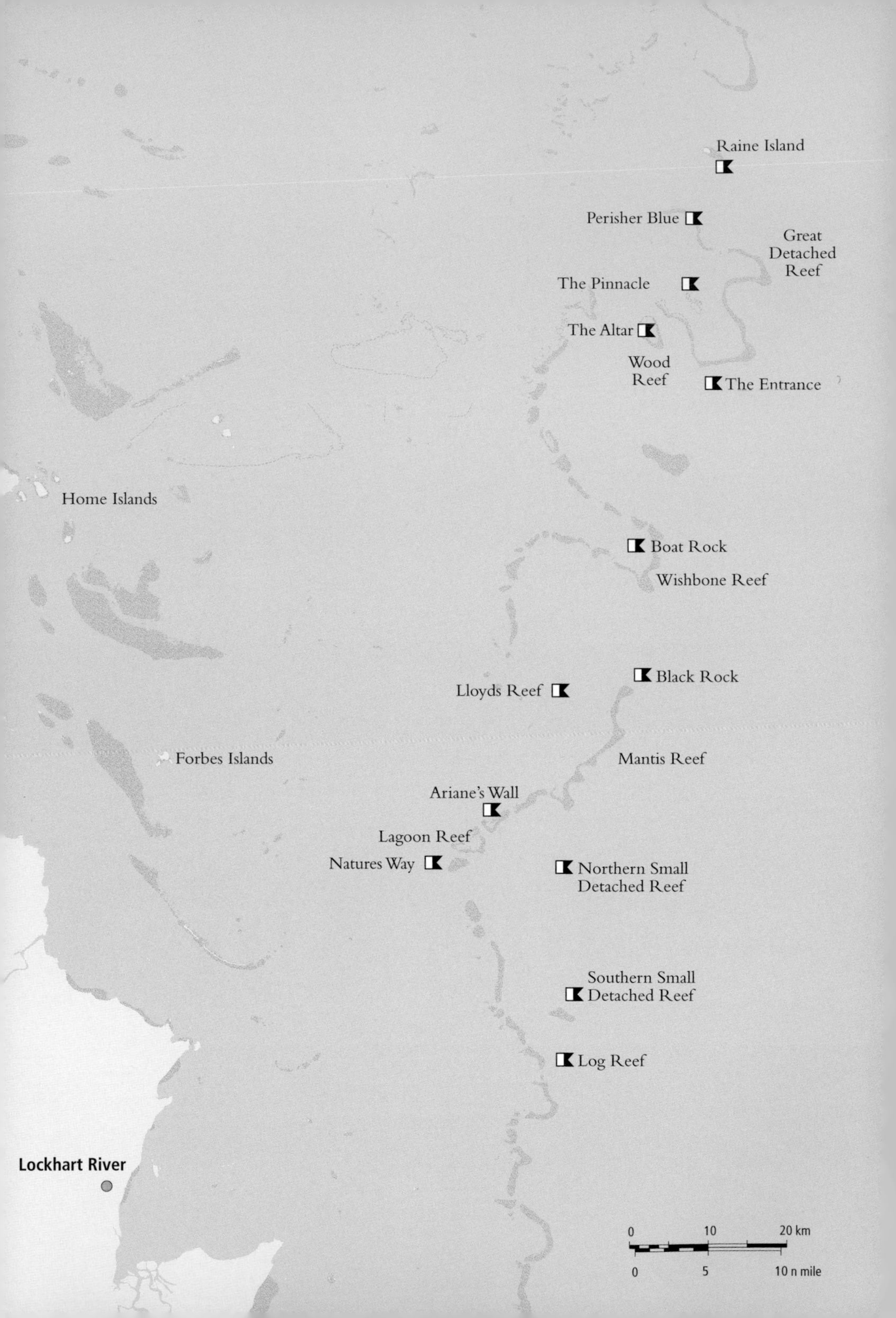

Raine Island

Perisher Blue

Great
Detached
Reef

The Pinnacle

The Altar

Wood
Reef

The Entrance

Home Islands

Boat Rock

Wishbone Reef

Lloyds Reef

Black Rock

Forbes Islands

Mantis Reef

Ariane's Wall

Lagoon Reef

Natures Way

Northern Small
Detached Reef

Southern Small
Detached Reef

Log Reef

Lockhart River

0		10		20 km

0		5		10 n mile

FAR NORTHERN REEFS

The northern section of the Great Barrier Reef is a long way from anywhere and mostly unexplored. However, this remote area, known as the Far Northern Reefs, offers the diver some of the most exciting diving to be found anywhere on the planet.

The Far Northern Reefs start at the top end of the Ribbon Reefs and continue north for another 600km to finish in waters that are closer to Papua New Guinea than Australia. Only accessible on a long range liveaboard boat, this area is blessed with an astonishingly diverse range of dive sites and marine life. Sheer walls, towering pinnacles, immense caves and beautiful coral gardens are just some of the terrain that can be experienced. Plus divers will encounter schools of pelagic fish, turtles, gropers and a large number of sharks.

Liveaboard charter boats generally only explore this area in November and December, as this time of the year has the most stable weather in this remote region. The boats often depart from Portland Roads, which is little more than a wharf close to the town of Lockhart River, about 800km north of Cairns. From here it is only a short hop into the heart of the incredible Far Northern Reefs.

Raine Island is the most iconic dive site of the Far Northern Reefs and for a very good reason. This remote island plays host to the largest green turtle rookery in the world, with thousands of turtles coming ashore at peak times to lay eggs in the island's warm sand. You can guarantee a turtle encounter at Raine Island, but with sheer walls dropping into deep water all around this amazing island there is much more than just turtles to be seen.

Wonderful soft corals, wide gorgonians, slender sea whips and bushy black coral trees adorn the walls all around Raine Island, and divers will also find plenty of caves and crevasses to explore. But it is the fish, turtles and sharks that most divers come to see. Pelagic fish constantly cruise these walls, with schools of trevally, barracuda, surgeonfish, drummer, batfish, snappers, fusiliers and rainbow runners to be seen. But large Spanish mackerel, giant trevally and

dogtooth tuna also patrol the depths. Turtles are everywhere, relaxing on the wall, swimming in the blue or lazing on the surface. If you are lucky you may even see a pair mating.

However, many divers come to Raine Island just to see sharks, as whitetip reef sharks, blacktip reef sharks, grey reef sharks and silvertip sharks are all very common. But the tiger sharks are the big draw card, as they hang around Raine Island feeding on the sick, injured and tired turtles. These large sharks patrol the wall and shallows, but are not often seen by divers as they are wary of bubbles. Raine Island is a very spectacular dive site.

Great Detached Reef covers such a large area and has so many dive sites that it could be a dive destination solely by itself. With walls on its eastern side and a large lagoon full of bommies on its western site it would take a lifetime to explore this reef. **Perisher Blue** is a lovely dive site at the northern end of Great Detached Reef with coral gardens in the shallows and a sandy bottom sloping into deep water. Whitetip reef sharks and blacktip reef sharks are common at this site, along with pelagic fish like mackerel, trevally and barracuda. The clean white sand at this site looks like snow and is home to a large colony of garden eels. But don't forget to check-out the shallow coral gardens as sweetlips, coral trout, moray eels and a great variety of reef fish and invertebrates live here.

The western side of Great Detached Reef is a deep water lagoon that is dotted with countless bommies, one of the best is simply called **The Pinnacle**, and is a giant tower of coral rising from 40m to 4m. Swimming circuits around this large bommie divers can admire the wonderful coral growth, look for macro subjects or just study the fish life. Expect to see nudibranchs, pipefish, lionfish, moray eels, anemonefish, flatworms, shrimps, crabs and larger species like grey reef sharks, rainbow runners, parrotfish, snappers, sweetlips and turtles.

At the southern end of Great Detached Reef is a wall of coral at a spot called **The Entrance**. The wall is worth a quick look as reef sharks and pelagic fish cruise here, but for the best action let the current suck you into the lagoon. Divers can drift along a channel wall that drops into 30m and is decorated with beautiful gorgonians, soft corals, black coral trees and sea whips. You can also zoom along the bottom of the channel, just watch out for the bommies that loom out of the sand. Cruising in the current with you will be jobfish, trevally, dogtooth tuna, reef sharks, turtles, gropers, barracuda, Maori wrasse and many other species.

OPPOSITE TOP: A dazzling array of small damselfish shelter in the hard corals on the Far Northern Reefs.

OPPOSITE BOTTOM: Red spotted porcelain crabs live in sea anemones. They are not a true crab and actually feed on plankton that they capture with feather-like jaw legs.

OVERLEAF: The spine-cheek anemonefish is bold and always really for a fight to defend its sea anemone, even attacking divers if they get too close.

At Wood Reef is a spectacular dive site called **The Altar**. Located on a peninsula at the western tip of the reef this site features coral walls and an incredible cave. This wide cave cuts right through the point, from one side to the other, and is lined with the most exquisite corals – soft corals, gorgonians, sea whips and black corals. Divers have to be very careful where they place their fins as you wouldn't want to damage any of these corals. Beside the cave there is also a plateau at the point where schools of fish and sharks mingle. At The Altar divers will see reef sharks, gropers, humphead parrotfish, trevally, mackerel, moray eels and silvertip sharks.

Off the western side of Wishbone Reef are numerous bommies rising from 30m of water. A large boat-shaped bommie, called **Boat Rock**, is a ripper of a dive on this reef, especially when a current is running. Almost 20m tall, Boat Rock is covered with beautiful corals and good place to see masses of reef fish. Maori wrasse, snappers, fusiliers, parrotfish, emperors, angelfish, reef sharks and a wide assortment of invertebrate species make this a special site.

Mantis Reef is a long reef with many options, but the best of them is at the northern tip and is called **Black Rock**. This is one of the most popular dive sites on the Far Northern Reefs as the wall here is always loaded with life. At Black Rock divers explore a sloping wall that disappears into 40m plus. Sharks are a constant companion at this site, so expect to see all the usual reef sharks and a few large silvertip sharks. The deeper sections of this wall are adorned with lovely gorgonians and soft corals which are very photogenic. Usually washed by currents, Black Rock is also a good location to see mackerel, dogtooth tuna, barracuda, trevally, jobfish, turtles and even queenfish and cobia. The coral gardens in the shallows shouldn't be forgotten as lionfish, garden eels, stingrays and a great assortment of reef fish reside here.

On the western side of **Lloyds Reef** is a group of bommies that are home to large quantities of fish. Rising from 25m to 3m, divers can explore gutters and caves to see reef sharks, turtles, Maori wrasse, trevally, sweetlips and fusiliers. The coral here is worth a close inspection as cuttlefish, nudibranchs, flatworms, porcelain crabs and many featherstars containing squat lobsters and clingfish, can be seen.

Off North Lagoon Reef is a wonderful dive site known as **Ariane's Wall**. Dropping from just below the surface to 35m this wall is coated in pretty corals

OPPOSITE TOP: Lovely red whip corals decorate the bommies and walls of the Far Northern Reefs.

OPPOSITE BOTTOM: Forster's hawkfish are usually observed propped on a coral outcrop and watching the world go by.

and home to a great range of reef fish and invertebrates. Humphead parrotfish, reef sharks, snappers, Maori wrasse, gropers and turtles are some of the species seen here. This wall seems to be a site where parrotfish spawn, so keep an eye out for groups of these fish rising into midwater and releasing eggs and sperm.

At South Lagoon Reef is another brilliant wall dive called **Nature's Way**. Similar to Ariane's Wall, with many of the same species, a highlight of this site is a shallow sandy bay dotted with coral heads. This bay is full of garden eels, and is also a good spot to see reef sharks, turtles and broadclub cuttlefish. It also makes for an entertaining night dive with shrimps, crabs, nudibranchs, flatworms, soles and numerous molluscs species to be seen.

Northern Small Detached Reef rises from depths of 200m to just below the surface. All around this dramatic reef are sheer walls dropping into deep water. Colouring the walls are large gorgonians and black coral trees, and divers will find plenty of caves to investigate. Pelagic fish constantly circle this isolated reef; trevally, mackerel, barracuda, dogtooth tuna and the ever present reef sharks. But sitting out in the middle of nowhere just about anything can cruise by, a marlin, whale shark or even a hammerhead.

The walls around **Southern Small Detached Reef** are even more spectacular, disappearing into 400m of water. Just about anywhere you dive around this reef you will see wonderful corals, heaps of fish and sharks. Grey reef sharks and silvertip sharks are quite common, as are large Maori wrasse, gropers, sweetlips and snappers. But it's not all walls here as there are a few sandy bays in the shallows where whitetip reef sharks, giant clams and even the odd leopard shark can be seen.

At **Log Reef** divers can do a magic drift dive along a coral wall off the northern end of the reef. Barracuda, reef sharks and Maori wrasse patrol this wall, along with mackerel, turtles and schools of parrotfish. This lovely site is also home to a giant Queensland groper and a good place to see cuttlefish.

There are many other wonderful dive sites on the Far Northern Reefs, way too many to fit into this book. But the dive sites listed above are just a sample of the incredible diving that can be experienced in this remote region of the Great Barrier Reef.

OPPOSITE TOP: Featherstars come in an amazing variety of colours and many play host to small commensal species like squat lobsters and clingfish.

OPPOSITE BOTTOM: Many fish species hide amongst the corals, such as these scaly damselfish, but emerge to feed on passing plankton.

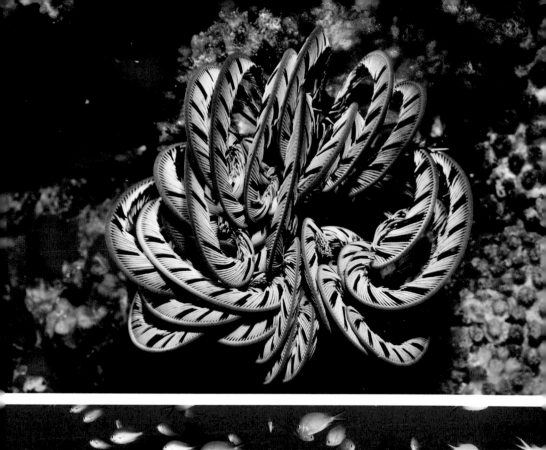

FAR NORTHERN REEFS DIVE DATA

HOW TO GET THERE – A liveaboard charter boat is the only way to explore the Far Northern Reefs. Boats generally depart from either Portland Roads or Cairns depending on the itinerary, so a flight to or from the Lockhart River (only a few kilometres from Portland Roads) is included as part of the charter. Cairns Airport is the major gateway to north Queensland, serviced by both domestic and international flights.

BEST TIME TO VISIT – The months of November and December are the only time of the year that charter boats visit this area.

VISIBILITY – 15m to 40m, depending on the reef and tides.

CURRENTS – Mild to strong, depending on the reef and tides.

WATER TEMPERTURE – In November and December it varies from 26°C to 28°C.

ABOVE: Giant thorny oysters are often found attached to walls and bommies in the Far Northern Reefs.

OPPOSITE: Countless species of coral are found on the Great Barrier Reef, they may vary in shape, size and colour, but they all have polyps which are used for feeding.

CAPE YORK SHIPWRECKS

A number of ships have come to grief in the Far Northern Reefs area, including two of the most famous shipwrecks in Australia.

RMS *Quetta* was a 120m long Royal Mail ship, launched in 1881. Owned by the British-India Steam Navigation Company the ship carried passengers and cargo between Brisbane and London. In 1890 the RMS *Quetta* was north of Cape York on a voyage to England when it hit an uncharted rock and sank. With 134 people lost in the sinking it is still the worst maritime disaster in Queensland history.

Today the RMS *Quetta* rests on its port side in 18m of water and is a spectacular dive. Covered in corals and home to gropers, sharks and masses of fish, many divers rate it as good or better than the SS *Yongala*. The wreck is largely intact, and divers can penetrate many sections of this large ship. Unfortunately the RMS *Quetta* is rarely dived as its remote location is well away from most of the reefs of the Far Northern Reefs.

The other famous shipwreck in this area is HMS *Pandora*, a 24 gun Royal Navy warship that was launched in 1779. Sent to Tahiti to capture the crew involved in the infamous 'Mutiny on the *Bounty*', the ship was returning to England with 14 prisoners. But on 28 August 1791 the ship ran aground and later sank just north of Raine Island.

HMS *Pandora* today rests in 35m of water and is mostly covered in sand. Several archaeological expeditions have recovered many historical items off this ship, but much of the shipwreck remains on the sea floor. A historic site, a special permit is required to dive HMS *Pandora*, so it rarely receives visitors.

North Horn

North Horn Wall

Castles

Silver City

Halfway Reef

Secret Caves

Admiralty

Round the Bend

False Entrance

Osprey Reef

0   4 km

0   2 n mile

Rapid Horn

OSPREY REEF

I f you want to see sharks, and lots of them, on your journey to the Great Barrier Reef, you are better off looking beyond the Great Barrier Reef to the remote waters of the Coral Sea. The Coral Sea Reefs offer the diver some of the most exciting adventure diving in the world, where sharks are a guarantee, especially at Osprey Reef.

Located 350km northeast of Cairns, Osprey Reef is the tip of an old mountain range and covers an area of 80 square kilometres. This remote reef is the most northern of all the Coral Sea Reefs and offers wonderful diving in its large lagoon and on the steep walls around its edge. Crystal clear water, steep walls that drop one kilometre, prolific reef fish, abundant pelagic fish and amazing over-sized corals make Osprey Reef a spectacular diving destination, but it is the sharks that most divers remember.

The only way to get to Osprey Reef is on a liveaboard dive boat. Fortunately Osprey Reef is the most regularly visited of all the reefs in the Coral Sea, with several charter boats visiting this remote reef each week. There are over a dozen dive sites at Osprey Reef, with most located on the north-western side of the reef, but the number one dive site here is the legendary **North Horn**.

Located at the very northern tip of Osprey Reef, North Horn is a sloping coral shelf fringed by walls that drop into 1000m of water. The shelf varies in depth from 12 to 45m, but has a natural amphitheatre that rises to 14m and is the location of the best shark feed in Queensland.

The liveaboard charter boats that visit Osprey Reef have been conducting shark feeds at this site for over thirty years. They don't hand feed the sharks, but instead remotely release a cage full of bait. Divers are arranged around the amphitheatre and look upon a central alter where the bait is to be released. As soon as the bait box hits the water the sharks, which are always present at this

OPPOSITE: Close encounters with whitetip reef sharks and other shark species are guaranteed at Osprey Reef.

57

location, rise to follow it to the bottom. Once in position the cage is opened, allowing the grey reef sharks and whitetip reef sharks to rip apart the baits in a savage display of aggression. The odd silvertip shark also joins in the feed, as do hundreds of red bass, fusiliers, common darts and several large potato cod.

The shark feed at North Horn is quite spectacular, but also chaotic and difficult to photograph. But this site is actually more fun when the sharks are not being fed. For a start the soft corals, especially beyond 30m, are stunning and huge, the biggest ones well over a metre tall. There are also some lovely gorgonian fans here. North Horn is also home to an abundance of reef fish, including coral trout, Maori wrasse, parrotfish, butterflyfish, angelfish, sweetlips, surgeonfish and many others. Pelagic fish constantly cruise this area, with barracuda, trevally, Spanish mackerel and dogtooth tuna all common. But the main attraction at North Horn are the sharks and gropers.

Over fifty grey reef sharks patrol North Horn, and since they are accustomed to divers they come in very close to check-you-out. Over a dozen whitetip reef sharks also call this site home, and they are so blasé about divers that they will even swim between your legs. There are also three very friendly potato cod that are happy to pose for your camera.

But that's not all as North Horn is the sort of place where just about anything can happen. Hammerhead sharks are regularly seen here, especially in deeper water, and over winter schools of scalloped hammerheads often appear. Divers have also encountered manta rays, marlin, tiger sharks, thresher sharks and even whale sharks at this wonderful dive site.

An easy swim west of North Horn is **North Horn Wall**. This sheer wall of coral drops into the abyss and is often done as a drift dive. Numerous ledges, caves and overhangs cut into this wall and the corals found here are just exquisite, especially the hanging soft corals that seem to come in every colour of the rainbow. Macro photographers will find a wealth of species to photograph, but you have to be prepared to search the nooks and crannies for flatworms, nudibranchs, thorny oysters, pipefish, hawkfish, lionfish and many other species. While diving North Horn Wall divers always need to keep an eye on the blue water behind, below and above, otherwise you will miss seeing barracuda, reef sharks, giant trevally, rainbow runners, mackerel and even the odd hammerhead.

At **Silver City** divers have a choice of exploring a maze of bommies or a series of caves. The bommies have the best coral and marine life, including large gorgonians, whip corals, soft corals, Maori wrasse, gropers, trevally and numerous

OPPOSITE TOP: Grey reef sharks are seen in abundant numbers all around Osprey Reef, but the biggest population hangs out at North Horn.

OPPOSITE BOTTOM: Wonderful corals adorn the sheer walls all around Osprey Reef.

reef fish, but the caves are also fun to investigate. As its name suggests, Silver City is a good spot to see silvertip sharks, but they are generally wary of divers.

Admiralty is named after a rather large and rather old admiralty anchor wedged in a gutter at this dive site at the southern entrance to Osprey Reef lagoon. In depths from 10m to 30m divers will find a jumble of bommies, gutters and caves to explore at Admiralty. Whitetip reef sharks are common here and often seen resting on the sandy bottom or sleeping in caves. Divers are also likely to see grey reef sharks, moray eels, lionfish, coral trout, trevally, surgeonfish, jobfish and snappers. The sandy bottom is well worth a look as not only are gobies and numerous molluscs found here, but also a large colony of garden eels. Admiralty is also a popular night dive where divers will see flatworms, octopus, shrimps, crabs, sleeping parrotfish and whitetip reef sharks looking for a late night snack.

One of the best dive sites at Osprey Reef is a spot called **Around The Bend**. Often done as a drift dive, this site has numerous gutters and bommies in depths between 15m and 30m. But the main feature is a bommie coloured by soft corals where manta rays get cleaned. At times two or three manta rays can be seen queueing up for this service, keeping an army of cleaner wrasse very busy. Of course the manta rays are not the only ones using this service, but they do tend to queue jump ahead of the other fish. While exploring Around The Bend divers are also likely to see whitetip reef sharks, grey reef sharks and a good collection of reef and pelagic fish.

There are many other lovely dive sites at Osprey Reef, including **Castles**, **Secret Caves**, **Halfway Wall** and **False Entrance**, but if you get the chance don't miss **Rapid Horn**. Located at the southern tip of Osprey Reef, Rapid Horn is another outstanding wall dive with plenty of action. The corals and reef fish are again wonderful, but divers will spend all their time watching the sharks cruise by. Many schooling fish gather at this site, expect to see barracuda, trevally, mackerel, snappers, sweetlips, humphead parrotfish and maybe a Maori wrasse. Rapid Horn can only be dived in very calm conditions, or when northerly winds are blowing over the summer months.

A few kilometres south of Osprey Reef is another Coral Sea Reef that can only be dived when conditions are calm, the amazing **Shark Reef**. This submerged reef, the highest point is about 8m, is a great place to see sharks and other large creatures of the deep.

Osprey Reef may be a little difficult to get to, and getting there involves a very bumpy overnight crossing, but it is well worth it to experience the spectacular diving in the Coral Sea and to see such healthy shark populations.

OPPOSITE: A number of resident potato cod can be observed at North Horn that are very accustomed to divers.

OSPREY REEF DIVE DATA

HOW TO GET THERE – Osprey Reef can only be visited on a liveaboard charter boat. Several of the boats operating out of Cairns visit this incredible reef on 4 day trips, combined with a day or two on the Ribbon Reefs. Some of these trips also visit a few of the other Coral Sea Reefs off Cairns, such as Bougainville Reef, Flora Reef and Holmes Reef. Cairns Airport is a major tourist gateway in north Queensland.

BEST TIME TO VISIT – Year round. But being so far offshore the open ocean crossing to Osprey Reef can be very rough. Trips are generally diverted to the Ribbon Reefs if the weather is too rough.

VISIBILITY – 30m to 50m.

CURRENTS – Generally mild.

WATER TEMPERTURE – Summer highs of 29°C to winter lows of 24°C.

– FEATURE –

COMMON SHARKS OF THE GREAT BARRIER REEF

The Great Barrier Reef is a great place to encounter a wide range of shark species. Over 70 species of shark have been recorded on the Great Barrier Reef, but many of these either live in deep water or are rarely seen. But the ones listed below are the sharks most often encountered by divers and snorkelers.

The most common shark seen in reef waters is the whitetip reef shark (*Triaenodon obesus*). These very distinctive looking sharks reach a length of 1.7m and are often observed sleeping on the bottom during the day. Studies have found that whitetip reef sharks have a strong site fidelity and have a home range of approximately 5km in diameter.

The grey reef shark (*Carcharhinus amblyrhynchos*) is another typical reef species that reaches a length of 2.5m. This species is more commonly seen on deeper reefs, especially walls, and are usually shy of divers. However they can be territorial at times, and have bitten a few divers, so be advised not to chase grey reef sharks.

Blacktip reef sharks (*Carcharhinus melanopterus)* are a small species that reach a length of 1.4m. They spend a lot of time in shallow water, especially on reef flats, so are often encountered by snorkelers.

BELOW: Whitetip reef shark.

OPPOSITE: Leopard shark.

Another shark that is commonly seen on reef flats, often in water less than a metre deep, is the epaulette shark *(Hemiscyllium ocellatum)*. This long slender shark grows to a metre in length and uses its fins to walk across the bottom.

Two of the largest sharks seen on the Great Barrier Reef are the harmless tawny nurse shark *(Nebrius ferrugineus)* and leopard shark *(Stegastoma fasciatum)*. The tawny nurse shark reaches a length of 3.2m and is often found sleeping in caves during the day. Leopard sharks, also known as zebra sharks, reach a length of 2.5m and are particularly common around the Capricorn and Bunker Groups.

The tasselled wobbegong *(Eucrossorhinus dasypogon)* is a well camouflaged shark of the reef and is often overlooked by divers. They reach a length of 1.2m and have a mouthful of very sharp teeth, but rarely bite unless harassed.

Another shark species commonly encountered on the outer reef and in the Coral Sea is the silvertip shark (*Carcharhinus albimarginatus*). This impressive shark reaches a length of 2.7m, but they are very wary of divers, especially the ones carrying cameras!

Many other shark species are seen in Great Barrier Reef waters, including whale sharks, thresher sharks, hammerhead sharks, bull sharks and tiger sharks, but encounters with these species is never guaranteed.

With shark numbers in decline around the planet due to fishing pressures it is great to see such a healthy shark population on the Great Barrier Reef. But the sad fact is that sharks are also fished on the Great Barrier Reef, and more protection is needed to ensure the future of these magnificent and important predators of the deep.

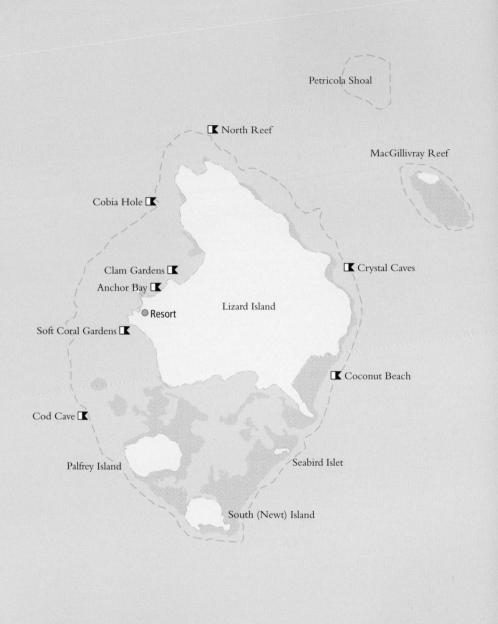

Petricola Shoal

North Reef

MacGillivray Reef

Cobia Hole

Clam Gardens

Crystal Caves

Anchor Bay

Resort

Lizard Island

Soft Coral Gardens

Coconut Beach

Cod Cave

Palfrey Island

Seabird Islet

South (Newt) Island

0   2 km

0   1 n mile

LIZARD ISLAND

Named for the giant monitor lizards that roam its shores, Lizard Island is renowned for being the location of one of Australia's most exclusive resorts. While close to some fabulous dive sites, including the world famous Cod Hole, most visitors to Lizard Island come to relax, unwind or chase after gamefish, with the nearby reef waters famous for record sized marlin. Lizard Island isn't a location that most budget conscience divers would ever consider visiting for a dive holiday, but if you have the money and want to be pampered, this picturesque island maybe just the place for you.

Lizard Island is situated 240km north of Cairns, and is one of four islands that make up the Lizard Island National Park. The island was named by Captain Cook in 1770, when he landed on its shores and climbed its highest peak, Cooks Look, to find a safe passage through the Great Barrier Reef. The island was later exploited for is abundant sea cucumbers in the 1860s, which lead to the Watson family settling on the island in 1879. Only nine months after establishing a home, Captain Watson was off gathering sea cucumbers when local Aboriginals attacked, killing one of the Watson's servants. Mrs Watson, another servant and her baby fled the island, only to die of thirst on a nearby island. Today the ruins of the Watson cottage can be seen, not far from the luxurious Lizard Island Resort.

Lizard Island Resort has 40 rooms, most of which overlook the blue waters that surround this lovely island. A dive centre is part of the resort facilities and they offer daily boat dives to the nearby dive sites around the island and to several sites around the Ribbon Reefs, which are around 20km away. With clear water lapping its shores and numerous rocky reefs to explore the diving around Lizard Island is very good. Schooling fish, gropers, sharks, turtles, sea snakes and rays are seen at most of the dive sites around Lizard Island.

Many liveaboard vessels visit Lizard Island as part of a trip to the Ribbon Reefs and Osprey Reef. They drop off and pickup passengers at the island, as it has an airstrip that services the resort. But these liveaboard boats rarely dive the sites around Lizard Island, which is a pity as they are by-passing some brilliant diving.

The best dive site at Lizard Island is the spectacular **Cobia Hole**. No bigger than a tennis court, this mound of boulders rises only a few metres above the surrounding sandy sea floor but is a haven for fish and other marine species. Going no deeper than 18m divers will find this reef decorated with pretty gorgonians, black corals and sea whips, and smothered in fish – red emperors, batfish, barracuda, trevally, barramundi cod, coral trout, sweetlips, coral cod, gropers and numerous colourful reef fish. The fish life at Cobia Hole can be staggering. But divers may also encounter turtles, whitetip reef sharks and sea snakes, and on the sand surrounding the reef have a look for stingrays and large cobia.

North Reef is a lovely wall dive with a good covering of soft corals, gorgonians, sponges and sea whips. In depths to 20m this wall attracts abundant marine life and also has many nooks and crannies to explore. Spotted eagle rays often cruise along the wall, alongside mackerel, trevally, fusiliers, batfish and turtles. But divers are also likely to encounter coral trout, gropers, moray eels and some colourful invertebrates like nudibranchs and shrimps.

Watsons Bay is a popular snorkelling spot as this shallow bay is dotted with coral heads. The **Clam Gardens** is a lovely dive site in this pretty bay, only 8m deep, but home to a wide variety of marine life. The bottom is dominated by hard and soft corals, that provide shelter for damsels, anemonefish, filefish, surgeonfish, butterflyfish and pufferfish. But larger fish are also common, with gropers, sweetlips, coral trout, barramundi cod, snappers and emperors all seen. As the name would suggest large clams are scattered around the reef, but divers will also see stingrays, moray eels, flatworms, nudibranchs, octopus, gobies and maybe a resting tawny nurse shark. **Anchor Bay** has similar terrain and marine life.

Macro photographers will have a field day at **Soft Coral Gardens**. This rocky reef off the western side of Lizard Island is only 10m deep but covered in radiant corals and home to a diverse range of reef fish and invertebrates. Photographers will find rock cods, grubfish, hawkfish, boxfish, pipefish, blennies, anemonefish, gobies, butterflyfish and lionfish to point their cameras at. Other photogenic subjects found on this site are nudibranchs, sea stars, flatworms, hermit crabs, cleaner shrimps and octopus.

OPPOSITE TOP: One of the most colourful fish seen on the Great Barrier Reef is the harlequin tuskfish.

OPPOSITE BOTTOM: Numerous seastar species are found in the waters around Lizard Island, include this nippled star.

Other brilliant dive sites around Lizard Island are **Coconut Beach**, **Cod Cave** and **Crystal Caves**. But the number one dive site off Lizard Island, and one of the best known dive sites in the world, is the wonderful Cod Hole, which is featured in the next chapter on the fabulous Ribbon Reefs.

LIZARD ISLAND DIVE DATA

HOW TO GET THERE – Lizard Island Resort has its own airstrip and most visitors to the island arrive via flights from Cairns, apart from those that arrive on their own boats. The flight takes around an hour and gives spectacular views of the Great Barrier Reef from the air. Lizard Island is also visited by liveaboard vessels venturing to the Ribbon Reefs, but they rarely dive the sites around the island.

BEST TIME TO VISIT – Year round.

VISIBILITY – 10m to 20m around the inshore dive sites.

CURRENTS – Generally mild.

WATER TEMPERTURE – Summer highs of 29°C to winter lows of 23°C.

BELOW: Exploring the many ledges and caves around Lizard Island divers will encounter coral rock cods.

OPPOSITE: Blue spotted lagoon rays are often seen at Lizard Island either resting under plate corals or grubbing in the sand for food.

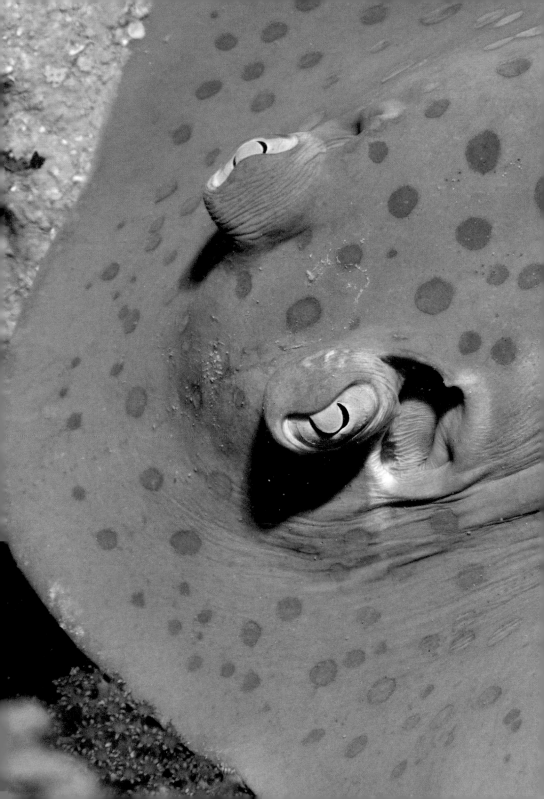

– FEATURE –
DANGEROUS REEF CREATURES

Many visitors to the Great Barrier Reef would consider an encounter with a shark as the main danger to their health. However, shark attacks are extremely rare and most sharks pose no threat to humans. The really dangerous creatures of the reef are much smaller, easily overlooked and fortunately easy to avoid.

One of the most deadly creatures of the Great Barrier Reef is a tiny mollusc, the cone shell. Numerous cone shell species are found in reef waters, but they are not often seen during the day as they are active at night. These highly venomous shells fire a poisonous dart to stun prey that is powerful enough to kill a human. Never pickup any cone shaped shell.

Always be careful around sea urchins, as being spiked by any species is painful, but some species are quite venomous and will leave you in intense pain. Also never touch a crown-of-thorns starfish as their spines are quite venomous. Sea snakes are also highly venomous, but not interested in biting a diver, and while stingrays have venomous spines on their tail, they rarely use them unless cornered or stepped on.

A number of venomous fish species inhabit the reef, including lionfish and other members of the scorpionfish family, but the most deadly of these are the stonefish. Looking just like a rock, stonefish are well camouflaged and rarely seen, but with a row of venomous spines they should never be touched.

Sea jellies (or jellyfish) are often found in reef waters, including the highly venomous irukandji and box jelly. These are more likely to be found in murky inshore waters than on the reef, but the best way to avoid being stung is to always wear a wetsuit or lycra suit.

Many anemones and corals can also sting if they come in contact with bare flesh, so cover up and just don't touch anything is the safest option.

While it may seem that there are many creatures on the Great Barrier Reef that can harm you, incidents are quite rare, with coral cuts from being careless the most common accident. But a little education can save you a lot of pain, and if you are stung by anything always seek immediate medical attention.

OPPOSITE TOP: Many species of cone shells are found in reefs waters, and none should ever be picked up or handled.

OPPOSITE MIDDLE: Ugly and highly venomous, the reef stonefish is not often seen by divers as they are very well camouflaged.

OPPOSITE BOTTOM: Many stingray species are found on the Great Barrier Reef like this blue spotted maskray. All possess a venomous barb, but usually pose little threat to divers unless harassed.

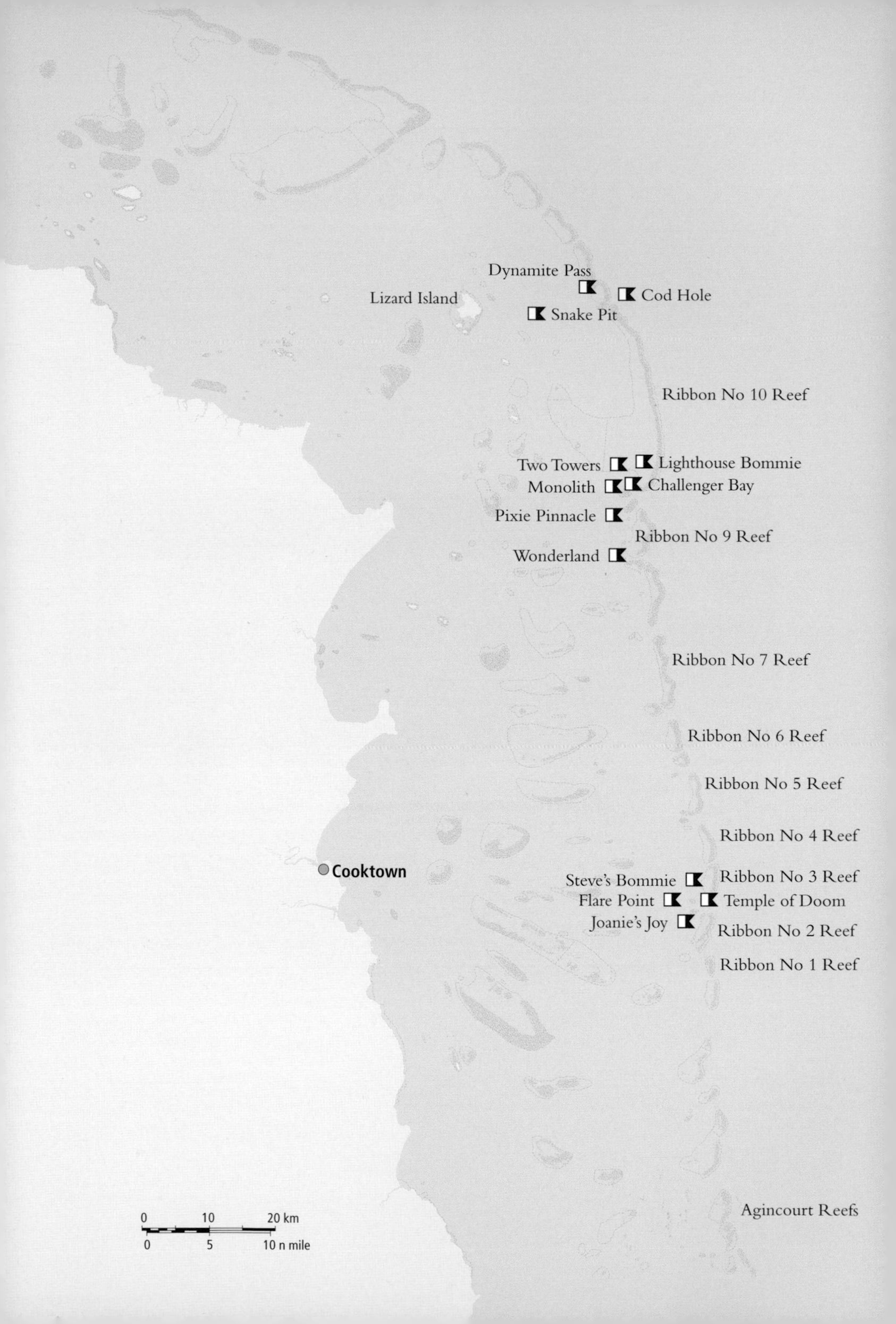

Dynamite Pass

Lizard Island

◨ ◨ Cod Hole

◨ Snake Pit

Ribbon No 10 Reef

Two Towers ◨ ◨ Lighthouse Bommie

Monolith ◨◨ Challenger Bay

Pixie Pinnacle ◨

Ribbon No 9 Reef

Wonderland ◨

Ribbon No 7 Reef

Ribbon No 6 Reef

Ribbon No 5 Reef

Ribbon No 4 Reef

Steve's Bommie ◨ Ribbon No 3 Reef

Flare Point ◨ ◨ Temple of Doom

Joanie's Joy ◨ Ribbon No 2 Reef

Ribbon No 1 Reef

● **Cooktown**

Agincourt Reefs

| 0 | 10 | 20 km |

| 0 | 5 | 10 n mile |

RIBBON REEFS

The Ribbon Reefs are a string of barrier reefs, north of Cairns, which stretch for over 100km. The outer edge of these reefs face ocean swells from the Coral Sea and are rarely dived, but the inner side is sheltered and offers an endless variety of pretty coral gardens, sloping walls and fantastic pinnacles packed with marine life. It is easy to see why this area is one of the most popular diving destinations on the Great Barrier Reef.

There are over one hundred dive sites located along the length of the Ribbon Reefs, and new sites are still being discovered all the time. All the dive sites on the Ribbon Reefs have something in common; masses of reef fish, healthy colourful corals and a wealth of invertebrate species. Diving the Ribbon Reefs you are also likely to see sea snakes, schooling pelagic fish, reef sharks, stingrays, gropers, turtles, cuttlefish and over the winter months something very special found nowhere else in the world – dwarf minke whales. All these attractions make the Ribbon Reefs an exceptional place to dive.

Probably the most famous dive site on the entire Great Barrier Reef is **Cod Hole**. This pretty reef, with its sandy gutters, ledges and coral gardens, is famous for its resident population of rather large and rather friendly gropers, known as potato cod. This fantastic dive site, on the northern end of Ribbon Reef No.10, was discovered in 1973 by Australian diving legends Valerie and Ron Taylor. They recognised how unique these friendly gropers were and fought to get the site protected from fishers, achieving their goal in 1981. Today these gropers are probably the most photographed fish on the planet.

The dive boats that visit Cod Hole regularly feed the gropers, which can be quite a show. But even without food in the water these giant fish are extremely friendly and curious, allowing divers to get eyeball to eyeball for some stunning images. When first discovered there were about 25 potato cod at the site, but today divers are likely to see anywhere from two to a dozen.

Cod Hole is a brilliant dive site where divers will see much more than

gropers, in depths from 3m to 36m the terrain at this site entices a wealth of marine life. Commonly seen are flowery gropers, coral trout, Maori wrasse, red bass, barramundi cod, whitetip reef sharks, moray eels, grey reef sharks, turtles, stingrays, cuttlefish, sweetlips, schools of humphead parrotfish and a wide variety of reef fish. A passing parade of pelagic fish includes barracuda, mackerel, trevally and fusiliers. For those after macro subjects there are nudibranchs, flatworms, anemonefish, scorpionfish, shrimps and coral crabs. Cod Hole is a dive site you will want to do again and again and again.

One of the most exciting dives on the Ribbon Reefs is a drift dive at **Dynamite Pass**. Located in the channel at the top of Ribbon Reef No.10, Dynamite Pass is at its best when a strong current is flowing. Divers glide along the coral wall watching a range of pelagic fish zoom pass; like barracuda, Spanish mackerel, bonito, giant trevally, jobfish and fusiliers. The wall itself is very colourful and home to reef fish, invertebrates, gropers, coral trout and Maori wrasse. Whitetip reef sharks are often observed, but if you are lucky you might also encounter spotted eagle rays, grey reef sharks or a manta ray.

If you don't like sea snakes then you would be best advised to avoid **The Snake Pit**. Located on the inner side of Ribbon Reef No.10, the twin bommies at The Snake Pit are home to around a dozen olive sea snakes. They are generally encountered swimming across the bottom and are interesting to watch as they search holes in the reef for prey.

The Snake Pit is an interesting dive site that varies in depth from 8m to 33m. The terrain at the site varies greatly; there are walls, bommies, coral gardens and sand flats to explore. Prolific marine life gathers at this site and divers will see Maori wrasse, sweetlips, coral trout, barracuda, gropers, cuttlefish, snapper, batfish and numerous titan triggerfish that are best avoided if nesting. The Snake Pit is also a good spot to encounter turtles, stingrays, cuttlefish, eagle rays and reef sharks.

Lighthouse Bommie got its name because it looks like a towering lighthouse. This single column of coral rises from 25m to 6m and is a haven for marine life. At the base of the pinnacle are several smaller coral mounds that are worth exploring as they are usually engulfed with thousands of yellow-lined snapper. Divers are also likely to encounter olive sea snakes searching the ledges for prey.

Exploring the main bommie divers will find lionfish, reef-top pipefish,

OPPOSITE TOP: Cod Hole is one of the best dive sites on the Great Barrier Reef, made famous by the resident population of friendly potato cod.

OPPOSITE BOTTOM: Massive schools of snapper are seen at dives sites throughout the Ribbon Reefs.

rock cod, angelfish, butterflyfish and a variety of nudibranchs. The walls of Lighthouse Bommie are decorated with soft corals, black coral trees, gorgonians and sea whips, which are a good place to find long-nose hawkfish and sea whip gobies. Just under the peak of the bommie is a wide shelf that leads to a cave that cuts right through the bommie. This cave is usually filled with squirrelfish and coloured by tubastra corals, and sometimes home to a large tasselled wobbegong shark. Safety stops at Lighthouse Bommie generally stretch beyond the required three minutes as divers are often mesmerised by a school of big-eye trevally swirling around them.

Lighthouse Bommie is located at the southern end of Ribbon Reef No.10, alongside a cluster of wonderful dive sites like **Two Towers** and **Monolith**. **Challenger Bay** is another brilliant dive site in this area where divers can explore coral gardens, small bommies and a sandy bay in depths from 6m to 30m. Challenger Bay is a great location to watch or photograph fish, as there are a number of cleaning stations here where very busy cleaner wrasse can be observed picking parasites and old skin from other fish. Commonly seen are sweetlips, triggerfish, moray eels, coral trout, fusiliers and rock cods. But this bay also attracts larger fish like barracuda, trevally, mackerel, Maori wrasse and schools of humphead parrotfish. A close look at the corals at this site will reveal abundant invertebrate species, including flatworms, feather stars, sea stars, nudibranchs and molluscs. Don't forget to have a look at the sandy bay as stingrays, whitetip reef sharks, gobies and sea cucumbers are common here, and the sand is also home to garden eels which sway back and forth with the surge.

Pixie Reef is a small reef located between Ribbon Reef No.9 and No.10. It has several wonderful dive sites located around its length, including **Pixie Wall** and **Pixie Garden**, but its best dive site is a coral skyscraper known as **Pixie Pinnacle**.

Pixie Pinnacle is one of the prettiest dive sites on the Ribbon Reefs. Rising from 35m to 4m, this lovely pinnacle is coloured by beautiful gorgonians, sponges and soft corals. It is particularly well known for its smaller critters – leaf scorpionfish, pipefish, nudibranchs, flatworms, commensal shrimps, hermit crabs, anemonefish, hawkfish and many more. A special feature are the flaming file shells, which hide in the ledges and flash incredible neon colours. But Pixie Pinnacle isn't just about the small stuff as it is also home to gropers, turtles, stingrays, reef sharks and pelagic fish. Pixie Pinnacle is also a brilliant night dive,

OPPOSITE TOP: Giant elephant ear sponges decorate many of the bommies of the Ribbon Reefs.

OPPOSITE BOTTOM: Steve's Bommie is a magnet for fish, with many different schools of fish on show.

the colours of the corals are radiant under torch light and a whole army of nocturnal critters emerge to feed, including coral crabs, decorator crabs, shrimps and octopus.

Located on Ribbon Reef No.9 the coral gardens at **Wonderland** form a lovely coral maze that is a joy to explore. The corals at this site are just beautiful and include radiant soft corals, slender sea whips and lovely patches of gorgonians. Divers can spend a lot of time searching between the corals for small critters like squat lobsters, nudibranchs, flatworms, gobies, commensal shrimps and anemonefish. There are also numerous caves at this site where lionfish and batfish reside, but always keep an eye on the blue water for passing pelagic fish like barracuda, trevally and mackerel. Wonderland is also a good spot to watch spotted eagle rays as they fly gracefully up and down the reef, but these rays can be quickly forgotten if their larger relative, the majestic manta ray makes an appearance.

The next cluster of great dive sites is found on Ribbon Reef No.3, these sites include **Flare Point**, **Joanie's Joy** and **Temple of Doom**, but the best of them is a tower of coral called **Steve's Bommie**. Although Steve's Bommie rises from 30m to 3m, many divers never get below 10m at this site as they are too preoccupied watching all the fish in the shallows. This amazing bommie is one of the fishiest dive sites on the Great Barrier Reef. Swarming around the top of the bommie are thick schools of big-eye trevally, yellow-fin goatfish, yellow-lined snapper, surgeonfish, batfish, fusiliers and chevron barracuda. The fish can be so dense at times that divers can lose sight of their buddy.

If divers can drag themselves away from the schooling fish there is plenty more to see at Steve's Bommie. The bommie is coated with pretty corals and sponges, and home to gropers, reef sharks, sea snakes, stingrays, eagle rays, moray eels, turtles and a range of reef fish. But this large bommie is also a macro photographers dream; mantis shrimps, reef stonefish, hawkfish, leaf scorpionfish, pipefish, anemonefish, lionfish, porcelain crabs, squat lobsters, flaming file shells and boxfish are just some of the species found on Steve's Bommie.

There is just so much to see on the Ribbon Reefs that it is understandable why divers come back year after year to explore more of this wonderful area.

OPPOSITE: A common sight on the Ribbon Reefs is swirling schools of big-eye trevally.

RIBBON REEFS DIVE DATA

HOW TO GET THERE – The top end of the Ribbon Reefs are visited by day boats from Lizard Island, but the only way to really explore this vast area is on a liveaboard boat. Several liveaboards based in Cairns visit the Ribbon Reefs each week, with some of the trips combining a visit to Osprey Reef. These trips vary in length from three to seven days, and some drop you at Lizard Island for a flight back to Cairns, which gives you a spectacular view of the reefs you have just dived. Cairns Airport is the major gateway to north Queensland and is regularly serviced by domestic and international flights.

BEST TIME TO VISIT – Year round, but June and July are the best months for dwarf minke whale encounters. The inner side of the Ribbon Reefs is shelter from strong winds and rough seas, and can still be dived quite comfortably with the wind blowing over 30 knots.

VISIBILITY – 20m to 30m.

CURRENTS – Usually mild to non-existent at most dive sites on the Ribbon Reefs, but there are strong currents in the channels between reefs which are often done as drift dives.

WATER TEMPERTURE – Summer highs of 29°C to winter lows of 24°C.

THE FRIENDLY WHALE

Encountering a whale underwater is an unforgettable experience, but also very rare unless you dive the Ribbon Reefs over the winter months. From March to October each year dwarf minke whales (*Balaenoptera acutorostrata*) gather on the Ribbon Reefs and they are the only whale species that seems to seek out the company of divers.

The dwarf minke whale is the smallest of the baleen whales, but still manages to reach 8m in length. These amazing little whales spend the summer months feeding in Antarctica and migrate to warm waters over winter to breed. Although seen elsewhere on the Great Barrier Reef, the best place to see minke whales is on the Ribbon Reefs, and the optimum time is June and July.

The dwarf minke whale is a very curious cetacean and enjoys the company of boats and divers, which has allowed the charter boats operating from Cairns to offer special minke whale trips each winter. All minke whale encounters happen on the whale's terms and regulations are in place to ensure that the whales are not harassed.

Once a whale approaches a dive boat ropes are put into the water and divers enter with snorkelling gear only. Holding onto the rope means that the divers are not moving about, allowing the whale to come in very close to see the bizarre rubber-clad beings. It is an unforgettable experience to have a 6m long whale swimming around you, and even more unforgettable if there are a dozen whales.

Dwarf minke whale encounters can last from minutes to hours to days, and often the divers exit the water cold and exhausted well before the whale gets bored. A minke encounter is one of the most magical experiences you will ever have on the Ribbon Reefs.

Agincourt Reef 4

Harry's Bommie ▐◀
Three Sisters ▐◀
The Chapel ▐◀

The Point ▐◀
▐◀ The Gap

▐◀ Wreck Bay
Turtle Bommie ▐◀
Two Rocks ▐◀

Agincourt Reef 3

Barracuda Bommie▐◀
Agincourt Reef 2
Phil's Reef ▐◀

Turtle Bay ▐◀   ▐◀
Nursery
Bommie

Agincourt Reef 1

Castle Rock ▐◀

St Crispin Reef

0   5 km
0   1   2 n mile

PORT DOUGLAS

Port Douglas is lovely holiday town north of Cairns, and the gateway to the wonderful Agincourt Reefs. The forty minute drive north of Cairns, along the Captain Cook Highway, this is one of the most scenic driving routes in Queensland, with spectacular views of the coastline, putting the visitor in a relaxed frame of mind for enjoying the Port Douglas area.

There are many attractions around Port Douglas. Head west and you have the spectacular Mossman Gorge. Head north and you can explore the Daintree Rainforest. But most visitors head east to visit the Great Barrier Reef, as not far off the coast of Port Douglas is the beautiful Agincourt Reefs.

While there are actually dozens of wonderful reefs off Port Douglas, the Agincourt Reefs are by far the most popular destination for day boats. Located on the continental shelf, the diving on the Agincourt Reefs is simply superb and almost as good as the neighbouring Ribbon Reefs.

The Agincourt Reefs are over 20km long and split into four sections. The eastern side of these reefs are rarely dived as they are exposed to ocean swells, but on the western side are lovely coral gardens, walls and numerous pinnacles to explore that are packed with marine life.

Harry's Bommie is located on Agincourt Reef No.4, at the northern end of this reef system, and is a great spot to see grey reef sharks. It is thought that the scattered bommies at this site are a nursery area for juvenile grey reef sharks. Harry's Bommie is only 16m deep, but divers will have a lot of fun exploring the coral gardens and coral outcrops at this site. All the typical reef fish are on display here, but divers should also keep an eye out for whitetip reef sharks, gropers and also the occasional manta ray.

There are a number of other wonderful dive sites on the western side of Agincourt Reef No.4, including **Three Sisters** and **The Chapel**, but **The Point** is a site that both divers and snorkelers will love. Located at the southern end of the reef, the dive at this site starts in a lagoon full of beautiful hard corals and overflowing with reef fish. Divers then swim around the point to find a lovely wall that drops to 30m. Currents flow along this wall, encouraging the growth of glorious soft corals, but it also attracts pelagic fish and other creatures. Cruising this wall are usually grey reef sharks, whitetip reef sharks, trevally, mackerel and barracuda. But also common here are flowery gropers, sweetlips, snappers and Maori wrasse.

The eastern side of the Agincourt Reefs is rarely dived, but there is one sheltered spot off Agincourt Reef No.3 that is worth a look called **Wreck Bay**. Named after a fishing boat that sunk here years ago, Wreck Bay varies in depth from 10m to 22m and is dotted with numerous bommies and some lovely coral gardens. A family of clown anemonefish are a popular photo stop at this site, but divers will also find some very photogenic diagonal-banded sweetlips hovering in groups. Wreck Bay is also a good place to see reef sharks, turtles, schools of drummers and goatfish, and with numerous ledges and caves in this area don't be surprised if you encounter a sleeping tawny nurse shark.

The Gap, **Turtle Bommie** and **Two Rocks** are other popular dive sites on Agincourt Reef No.3, but for a very relaxing dive have a look at **Phil's Reef**. Like many of the dive sites on the Agincourt Reefs, this site is dominated by lovely hard corals in depths to 22m. Often done as a drift dive, keep an eye out for nudibranchs, pipefish, coral trout, moray eels, tuskfish and boxfish as you fly over the lovely corals at Phil's Reef. Turtles and stingrays are also common at this site, and if you are really lucky you might see a broadclub cuttlefish or two.

Agincourt Reef No.2 has some of the best dive sites in this area, as numerous large bommies rise from the sandy lagoon on the western side of this reef, and each attracts a wealth of marine life. **Barracuda Bommie** rises from 26m to almost touch the surface. This giant tower of coral is a fabulous dive as it is coloured by gorgonians and soft corals, and covered in fish life. Swarming all over this bommie are schools of snappers, sweetlips, fusiliers, trevally, drummer and of course barracuda. If you can drag yourself away from all the fish the sand around the base of the bommie is worth checking out as stingrays, shrimp gobies and garden eels reside here. But Barracuda Bommie is also a good spot to see turtles, Maori wrasse, parrotfish, surgeonfish, fairy basslets, coral trout and many other species.

OPPOSITE, CLOCKWISE FROM TOP LEFT: A close inspection of sea anemones will often reveal dozens of tiny commensal shrimps; nudibranchs are common on the Great Barrier Reef, but sometimes difficult to find. Look for them around sponges and ascidians, their preferred diet; Barracuda Bommie is generally a great place to see mixed schools of pelagic fish, including snappers, batfish and barracuda; diagonal-banded sweetlips are often encountered by divers on the Agincourt Reefs.

Turtle Bay is another brilliant dive site on Agincourt Reef No.2 where you are very likely to have a close encounter with a turtle. Both green and hawksbill turtles are seen at this site, either resting on the bottom or slowly swimming about. Turtle Bay is dotted with bommies in depths to 20m, but the coral gardens in the shallows are also well worth investigating. Expect to see giant clams, lionfish, fusiliers, sweetlips, gropers and the odd reef shark.

Another wonderful pinnacle on Agincourt Reef No.2 is **Nursery Bommie**. This lovely bommie rises from 25m and is decorated with black coral trees, sea whips and soft corals. As you swim circuits around Nursery Bommie have a close look at the ledges and cracks as these shelter lionfish, squirrelfish, nudibranchs, moray eels and leaf scorpionfish. The lower section of Nursery Bommie is usually swarming with snappers and sweetlips, while the top is engulfed by schools of drummer, trevally and barracuda.

One of the best dive sites on this reef system is found on Agincourt Reef No.1 and is called **Castle Rock**. Rising from 25m, Castle Rock is rather a plain pinnacle, but it is home to numerous reef and pelagic fish, including trevally, fusiliers, snappers and sweetlips. But its most famous resident is a very tame Malabar groper called Colin. This metre long fish follows divers around the pinnacle and is happy to pose for photos, in fact it is such a photo hog that it will stick its nose right onto your camera lens.

The best feature of Castle Rock is the spectacular coral gardens in the shallows. These are some of the best you will see on the Great Barrier Reef, a great collection of staghorn corals, plate corals and many other hard corals species – all healthy and unbroken. These coral gardens are also home to a wide range of fish species, including damselfish, butterflyfish, snappers, sweetlips, goatfish, rock cods and angelfish. This is a site that both divers and snorkelers will love, especially if a dwarf minke whale makes an appearance, as they visit this and a number of other sites on the Agincourt Reefs over the winter months.

It would take many weeks of day trips to explore the numerous dive sites off Port Douglas, but what you can experience in a few days will leave you wanting more of the wonderful Agincourt Reefs.

OPPOSITE TOP: A wonderful wall of soft corals decorates the bommie at Castle Rock.

OPPOSITE BOTTOM: Divers will see common lionfish at many of the dive sites around the Agincourt Reefs.

PORT DOUGLAS DIVE DATA

HOW TO GET THERE – Port Douglas is located 60km north of Cairns. Bus connections from Cairns Airport and the city are available. Numerous day boats depart from Port Douglas to the Agincourt Reefs and adjacent reefs, and a number also include hotel pickup (they will also do this from Cairns hotels for a small fee). Cairns Airport is the major gateway to explore north Queensland and is serviced by both domestic and international flights.

BEST TIME TO VISIT – Year round.

VISIBILITY – 15m to 30m.

CURRENTS – Generally only mild currents.

WATER TEMPERTURE – Summer highs of 29°C to winter lows of 24°C.

ABOVE AND OPPOSITE: Colin, the resident Malabar groper of Castle Rock, is very accustom to divers and is always happy to have his photo taken.

CHAMELEON OF THE REEF

Exploring the coral gardens on reefs north of Cairns divers are likely to encounter a number of invertebrate species, but the most colourful and entertaining of these are without doubt the broadclub cuttlefish (*Sepia latimanus*). Found throughout Southeast Asia, the broadclub cuttlefish is not often found on other parts of the Great Barrier Reef, but appear to be common on the Agincourt Reefs and Ribbon Reefs.

Reaching a length of 50cm and weighing up to 5kg, broadclub cuttlefish are often observed just hovering above the corals. Known as the chameleons of the sea, these amazing animals can change colour in an instant and often flash dazzling colours when displaying to other cuttlefish or hunting prey. Cuttlefish can also change the texture of their skin to help them camouflage with their background.

Broadclub cuttlefish have been observed mating on the Great Barrier Reef, the couple locked together in a tangle of tentacles. The female then gentle deposits her eggs between the corals and sadly dies after a short life span of only one year.

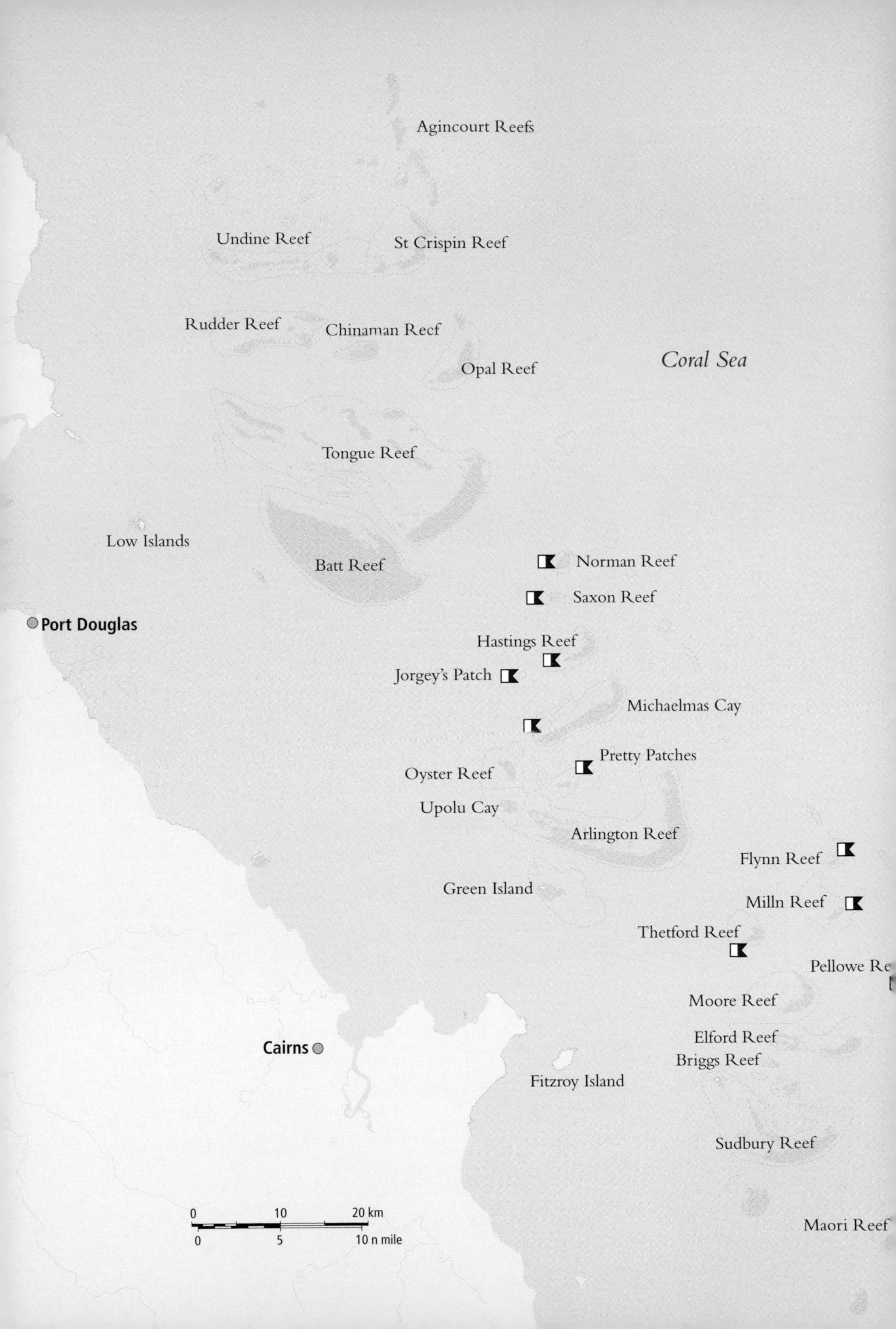

Agincourt Reefs

Undine Reef   St Crispin Reef

Rudder Reef   Chinaman Reef

Opal Reef   *Coral Sea*

Tongue Reef

Low Islands

Batt Reef   Norman Reef

                            Saxon Reef

Port Douglas

                    Hastings Reef

Jorgey's Patch

                                    Michaelmas Cay

                            Pretty Patches

Oyster Reef

Upolu Cay

Arlington Reef

                                            Flynn Reef

Green Island

                                            Milln Reef

                    Thetford Reef

                                        Pellowe Re

                    Moore Reef

Cairns

                            Elford Reef
                            Briggs Reef

            Fitzroy Island

                                    Sudbury Reef

0	10	20 km
0	5	10 n mile

                                    Maori Reef

CAIRNS

Many Australian divers have never explored the colourful reefs off Cairns as they live under the misguided assumption that these reefs have been ruined by hordes of tourist. But nothing could be further from the truth. While close to two million tourist a year visit the reefs off Cairns, the great majority of these visitors are either snorkelers that are happy to float on the surface or visitors that never enter the water in the first place, excited to view the coral from the comfort of a glass bottom boat. That is not to say that some careless divers don't break the coral at times, but there is little evidence of this at most dive sites.

Cairns if blessed with dozens of wonderful reefs on its doorstep that offer the diver and snorkeler a huge variety of dive sites to explore during a visit. On these reefs divers will find pretty coral gardens, a wealth of reef fish and a wide variety of invertebrate species. Some normally shy fish, like Maori wrasse, are so used to divers that they not only pose for photos but divers may have problems with them wanting to appear in every photo. Exploring the reefs off Cairns divers are also likely to see reef sharks, gropers, turtles, stingrays, pelagic fish and even the odd manta ray. Divers can explore the reefs off Cairns on day boats or from liveaboard vessels.

Norman Reef is the most northern of the reefs visited by charter boats from Cairns, around 70km northeast of the city. Located on the outer edge of the reef, Norman Reef is blessed with clear water, a great variety of dive sites and is sometimes visited by dwarf minke whales over the winter months.

One of the most popular dive sites at Norman Reef is the **Great Adventures Pontoon**, as a multitude of fish hang around this structure. In and around this pontoon divers can get up close and personal with trevally, barracuda, fusiliers, sweetlips, drummer, red bass, damsels and a very large and friendly Maori wrasse called Wally. There are also coral gardens to explore at this site, and you don't have to go any deeper than 15m.

A great variety of dive sites are located off the sheltered western side of Norman Reef. **First Bommie**, **Turtle Bay**, **Troppos**, **The Caves** and **Secret Garden** are just of few of these sites, and they are all quite similar with coral gardens and coral canyons in depths from 10m to 16m. At these sites divers will find anemonefish, batfish, stingrays, parrotfish, cuttlefish, coral trout, sweetlips, pipefish, turtles and a good selection of invertebrate species.

A night dive at **Playground** is a must do experience at Norman Reef. At night hundreds of large predator fish gather under the boat attracted by the lights (and a bit of food), common are big-eye trevally, giant trevally, red bass and occasionally a giant Queensland groper. But the action really heats up when the grey reef sharks arrive. Up to a dozen of these graceful sharks cruise around the fish and divers, weaving in and out of the light. Playground is one of the more spectacular night dives on the Great Barrier Reef.

Saxon Reef is another popular diving and snorkelling destination on the outer edge of the reef. **Magic Wall** is located at the northern end of Saxon Reef and is a pretty coral wall that drops from 6m to 20m. Exploring Magic Wall divers will encounter turtles, moray eels, whitetip reef sharks, sweetlips, coral trout, lionfish and schools of fusiliers. Take some time to admire the corals and investigate the nooks and crannies of the wall, as hidden here are sea stars, flatworms, commensal shrimps, hermit crabs, juvenile boxfish, blue tangs, pipefish and nudibranchs.

One of the best dives at Saxon Reef is called **Twin Peaks** and is located off the southwest corner of the reef. The two large pinnacles at this site rise from the sand at 22m to terminate just below the surface. Swimming circuits around these impressive pinnacles divers will see lovely whip corals, gorgonians and soft corals, plus a good variety of reef fish and invertebrates. Pelagic visitors are attracted to these pinnacles, with batfish, mackerel and trevally common. Other marine life seen at Twin Peaks can include whitetip reef sharks, blue-spotted stingrays, parrotfish, cuttlefish, snappers and gropers.

On the western side of Hastings Reef is a lovely dive site called **The Fish Bowl**. The coral gardens at this site vary in depths from 8m to 18m and feature patches of pretty staghorn corals and many anemones, some of which are occupied by clown anemonefish. Numerous giant clams litter the bottom at this site, but the fish life is the big attraction. Schools of fusiliers, snappers, goatfish, surgeonfish and parrotfish are common, but also seen are triggerfish, batfish, emperors, gropers and sweetlips. There is also a resident Maori wrasse at this site and manta rays have been known to drop in for a visit.

Off the southern end of Hastings Reefs is a wonderful wall dive known as **Wild Side**. This wall drops to 20m and is regularly visited by pelagic fish like trevally, barracuda, mackerel and rainbow runners. A number of small bommies rise from the sand at the base of this wall and they are well worth a look as they shelter sweetlips, coral trout and stingrays.

Jorgey's Patch is an inner reef that is not often dived, but it has fabulous corals and a good variety of reef fish. The most popular dive site here is **The Drop Off**, where divers can explore a wall that tumbles into 30m. With currents sweeping this wall pelagic fish are common, along with schools of snapper and fusiliers. Both whitetip reef sharks and grey reef sharks are seen at this site, but also keep an eye out for Maori wrasse, stingrays and sweetlips.

Michaelmas Reef has one of the few coral cays off Cairns, which is a nesting site for turtles and thousands of sea birds. While there are pretty coral gardens found off this reef, one of the best dive sites is right in front of **Michaelmas Cay**. In the shallows off the cay are coral heads, giant clams and countless reef fish. Turtles, blue-spotted lagoon rays, whitetip reef sharks, blacktip reef sharks, scorpionfish, grubfish and surgeonfish are all seen at this shallow dive site.

Pretty Patches is a small reef with its best dive site called **The Canyons**. As the name suggests this site is dominated by coral canyons in depths from 10m to 20m. Divers will encounter turtles, stingrays, sweetlips, fusiliers and a good collection of anemonefish while exploring this site.

Flynn Reef sits on the outer edge of the reef and has a number of wonderful dive sites along its southern side. At **Tracey's Bommie** divers will find a scattering of bommies in depths from 6m to 22m. Larger bommies are found out in deeper water, where pelagic fish, reef sharks and gropers are spotted. But some of the best diving is found in the shallows, as turtles, sweetlips, fusiliers and all manner of reef fish are found here.

One of the most interesting dive sites at Flynn Reef has the unimaginative name of **Public Mooring**. The terrain at this site has it all; gardens of hard coral in the shallows, a coral wall, numerous canyons and also plenty of bommies.

OPPOSITE TOP LEFT: Blennies are one of the smaller reef fish seen on the Great Barrier Reef. They like to hide amongst the coral and are rarely more than 10cm long.

OPPOSITE TOP RIGHT: Nudibranchs come in a wide variety of colours, and are common at the dive sites off Cairns.

OPPOSITE BOTTOM: Divers regularly encounter green turtles on the reefs off Cairns.

Divers can pick a depth to suit their experience level, as the reef here varies in depth from 6m to 30m. A family of Maori wrasse reside at this site and are happy to pose for photos, but divers will also see mackerel, trevally, barracuda, batfish, parrotfish and whitetip reef sharks. But this wonderful site also has many invertebrate species like commensal shrimps and nudibranchs.

Tennis Court is another popular site at Flynn Reef, with coral gardens in depths from 5m to 9m, a wall dropping to 20m and also a large sandy gutter cutting into the centre of the reef. Giant clams, anemonefish, reef sharks, stingrays, cuttlefish, sweetlips, nudibranchs and turtles are just some of the species seen.

Thetford Reef is a popular site close to Cairns that doesn't always have the clearest of water, but still has some interesting dive sites. **Tusa Canyons** has pretty coral gardens and a wall to explore in depths from 6m to 20m. Many caves and swim-throughs are found at this site, and divers will encounter sweetlips, triggerfish, coral trout, stingrays and abundant reef fish.

Horseshoe is a series of large bommies in depths from 10m to 25m. Deep gutters cut between these bommies where some beautiful gorgonians and sea whips can be found. Large fish like giant trevally, emperors, snappers and sweetlips are common, but other species seen here include moray eels, anemonefish, squirrelfish and cuttlefish.

Dog Bommie is one of the most spectacular sites at Thetford Reef, with this tower of coral rising from 22m to 4m. Decorated with exquisite corals, the main feature of Dog Bommie are pelagic fish, with large dogtooth tuna regular visitors.

The Wall is a pretty wall dive on the southern side of Thetford Reef. Dropping to 25m divers often encounter pelagic fish, reef sharks and eagle rays at this site, but also keep an eye out for the resident leopard shark.

Milln Reef has some of the most spectacular dive sites to be found off Cairns, with **Three Sisters** easily the best dive site in the area. This group of three towering pinnacles has it all – beautiful corals, dramatic terrain and loads of fish. These pinnacles rise from depths between 20m and 30m, but novice divers can still explore their tops. Large gorgonians, several metres wide, are a feature of this site as they sprout from the canyon walls between each pinnacle. But these pinnacles are also decorated with lovely whip corals, sponges, soft corals and sea whips. Turtles, reef sharks, red bass, mackerel, batfish, barracuda, stingrays and moray eels are just some of the common species. However, the main feature is the massive schools of fusiliers, snappers, sweetlips and drummers that engulf the tops of these pinnacles. This is a dive that will leave you breathless!

Another excellent site at Milln Reef is **Oasis**. This site has pretty coral gardens in the shallows and a maze of bommies in deeper water. It is easy to get lost at this site, and divers need to keep an eye on their depth as it is possible to reach depths of 30m. Oasis has a great collection of reef fish and invertebrate species, but divers will mostly enjoy seeing the schools of barracuda, snappers and fusiliers. Turtles, reef sharks and stingrays are also common at this brilliant dive site.

Pellowe Reef is another exiting dive site off Cairns with walls on its southern side dropping into 30m of water. Pelagic fish parade along this wall, and are often joined by reef sharks, Maori wrasse and eagle rays.

There are many other dive sites off Cairns, but sites like **Moore Reef**, **Briggs Reef** and **Elford Reef** are not visited as often as the sites listed above. Divers can also explore **Green Island** and **Fitzroy Island**; and while both of these sites having great marine life, they are closer to the mainland so often have poor visibility.

Cairns has such a great variety of dive sites and marine life it is easy to see why this city is the most popular gateway to the Great Barrier Reef.

CAIRNS DIVE DATA

HOW TO GET THERE – Cairns is the most popular holiday town in north Queensland and serviced by both international and domestic flights. Numerous day boats depart from Cairns each morning for a day on the reef, offering either two or three dives. Some of these visit the inner reefs and some the outer reefs, with the destination often determined by the prevailing winds and seas. The reefs off Cairns can also be explored on liveaboard vessels, with these trips generally two to four days in length, and allowing up to five dives a day.

BEST TIME TO VISIT – Year round.

VISIBILITY – 10m to 30m, with the clearest water on the outer reefs.

CURRENTS – Generally only mild currents.

WATER TEMPERTURE – Summer highs of 29°C to winter lows of 24°C.

— FEATURE —
REEF CARE

'Take nothing but photos, leave nothing but bubbles' is a great sentiment, but many divers have an impact on the Great Barrier Reef and some don't even realise it.

Before any dive on the Great Barrier Reef your dive guide will brief you on what to do, what you will see and will also point out that you shouldn't take anything, touch anything or damage anything. This may sound obvious, especially in a marine park, but it is amazing how many divers, and not just inexperienced beginners, ignore these simple rules through ignorance, stupidity or by accident. To help protect the corals and marine life of the Great Barrier Reef here are some simple things you can do or avoid.

Make sure you have good buoyancy control. If you are overweighted you are likely to crash into the bottom and damage the coral or yourself. Take a little time at the surface to make sure your weight is correct, and with good buoyancy you will be able to graceful glide over the corals without causing any damage.

Be aware of your fins at all times. As the fins are an extension of your feet it is often difficult to judge where they are, so try to keep them up and off the coral. If you kick the coral because your fins are below you, either move higher off the bottom or get into a horizontal position with your fins well off the bottom.

If you need to settle on the bottom to adjust your gear, find a sandy patch to kneel on. If you find yourself in a current or if you need to steady yourself to take photographs, don't rest your entire body on the coral, look for a dead piece of coral or a bare rock and hold onto it lightly with one hand, this should be enough to keep you in one place.

Please don't touch the marine life. While touching some animals will have no impact on them, others can die from shock or infections. So the simple rule is don't touch the marine life. Friendly potato cod and Maori wrasse are often seen with nasty skin infections from divers, who were briefed not to touch the animals, but touched them anyway! This rule is there to not only protect the marine life, but you as well as some animals can bite and others can sting.

At the end of the day divers really have minimal impact on the Great Barrier Reef, and even popular dive sites that are visited by hundreds of divers each week show little evidence of diver impact. Cyclones cause the greatest damage to the reef each year, wiping out entire reefs. But fortunately coral is very resilient and reefs quickly regenerate after only a few years. However, a little diver care can go a long way to ensuring the health of the Great Barrier Reef.

Osprey Reef

Shark Reef

0   100 km

0   50 n mile

Cooktown

Bougainville Reef

Willis Islets

Holmes Reef

Port Douglas

Herald Cays

Coringa Islets

Cairns

Diamond Islets

Herald's Surprise

Lihou Reef
and Cays

Flinders Reef

Boomerang Reefs

Abington Reef

NORTHERN CORAL SEA REEFS

The Coral Sea Reefs, beyond the Great Barrier Reef, are renowned as one of the most spectacular places to dive in the world. Sheer walls that drop a kilometre into the depths, giant pinnacles, enormous corals, incredible marine life, abundant sharks and some of the clearest water in the world make this area a very special dive destination.

The wonderful reefs of the Coral Sea are in fact the peaks of an ancient mountain range that disappeared at the end of the last ice age when sea levels rose to flood low lying areas. Today this immense area, covering 780,000 square kilometres, is a territory of Australia and, apart from a weather station on Willis Island, is uninhabited.

Thirty reefs and atolls are found in this enormous area (which actually extents much further south than the Great Barrier Reef, but this book only covers the area adjacent to the Great Barrier Reef), which is generally split into two regions, north and south. This division is mainly for convenience, but these areas actually have quite different diving, terrain and marine life.

The Northern Coral Sea Reefs encapsulates the very popular Osprey Reef (see page 57), but also includes a number of amazing reefs off Cairns and Townsville. These isolated reefs are only accessible on a liveaboard boat, and being over 200km offshore getting to them generally involves a rough overnight ocean crossing. But a little seasickness is a small price to pay for some of the most exciting diving on the planet.

Bougainville Reef is only 4km in diameter and quite exposed in rough conditions, so is usually only dived as a stop-off to other reefs in the area. However charter boats always like to stop here as it has some exceptional wall dives and a rather interesting shipwreck.

OPPOSITE: Divers should always take care when exploring caves and ledges as common lionfish are often hidden in the shadows.

North Wall is located at the northern end of Bougainville Reef and is a typical Coral Sea wall dive. Drop down below 30m if you want to see the best corals as large gorgonians, soft corals and black coral trees sprout here that are larger than most divers. But anywhere you dive along this wall you will find plenty of nooks and crannies to explore and a great range of reef fish and invertebrates. But off the wall is where the action is as cruising the blue are reef sharks, barracuda, surgeonfish, mackerel, trevally, gropers, Maori wrasse and large dogtooth tuna.

The top of Bougainville Reef has pretty coral gardens and also the wreck of the **MV *Antonio Tarabocchia***. This 140m long Italian freighter ran aground in 1961 and soon became a total wreck. The broken up ship makes for a great dive in depths from 6m to 18m, with wreckage scattered all over the place. Many reef fish shelter in the wreck, include the odd groper.

Holmes Reef is the closest Coral Sea Reef to Cairns, only 240km offshore, and has many exciting dive sites. The reef is split into two sections, known as West Holmes Reef and East Holmes Reef, and both have large lagoons that provide a safe anchorage for liveaboard boats. The most popular dive sites at Holmes Reef are found on the western section, where walls, pinnacles and caves can be explored.

Turbo is a spectacular pinnacle that rises from 35m. Usually washed by currents, this tower of coral teems with pelagic visitors, with schools of barracuda, trevally and rainbow runners common. Divers are also likely to encounter grey reef sharks, mackerel, surgeonfish and abundant reef fish on this lovely pinnacle.

Holmes Reef's most popular dive site is a giant bommie called **Nonki**. Japanese for 'easy going', Nonki is an easy dive where you can pick a depth to suit your experience. More experienced divers can drop down to 35m to explore caves and swim throughs. However, a feature of this site is an enormous crack that splits this pinnacle in two and is covered in pretty soft corals and incredible gorgonians. Tawny nurse sharks often shelter at this bommie, but divers are also likely to encounter lionfish, sweetlips, gropers and squirrelfish. But you don't have to go deep to have a good dive at this site as the top of the bommie is only 5m deep and usually engulfed by a school of big-eye trevally.

If you like cave diving **Amazing** is the site for you. The reef at this site is literally riddled with caves in depths 10m to 20m. While some of these caves are large and easy to find, the best caves have small entrances and should only

OPPOSITE TOP: Many beautiful butterflyfish are seen on the Great Barrier Reef and Coral Sea, including the lovely blue-dash butterflyfish.

OPPOSITE BOTTOM: While exploring the coral walls of the Northern Coral Sea Reefs divers are likely to encounter groups of tall-fin batfish.

be explored with a guide as they are very dark and quite narrow at points. A torch is a must, not only to see where you are going, but to light up the cave residents; squirrelfish, gropers, cardinalfish and a surprising number of crayfish. Less experienced divers, or those not interested in caves, will still enjoy a dive at Amazing, as there are attractive coral gardens and sweetlips, triggerfish, stingrays, surgeonfish and a colony of garden eels on the sand.

At the southern end of West Holmes Reef is a sheer wall dotted with numerous dive sites with names like **Golden Wall**, **The Cathedral** and **The Abyss**. The wall here drops into 1km of water and as you descend you will be looking down into darkness. Lovely corals decorate this wall, and pretty reef fish and invertebrate species are common, especially in all the ledges and caves, but the sharks and pelagic fish are the main attraction. Grey reef sharks patrol this wall, and divers will often see several at a time, also keep an eye out for whitetip reef sharks, silvertip sharks, turtles, mackerel, dogtooth tuna, barracuda and trevally. There are dozens of other brilliant dive sites at Holmes Reef and some of the charter boats even do a shark feed here at a site called Predators Playground.

ABOVE: Dense schools of chevron barracuda can be seen at many of the dive sites in the Northern Coral Sea.

Nearby **Flora Reef** is only dived when conditions are calm as this small reef offers little protection for charter boats as it is completely submerged. If you can dive here you will find gorgeous walls right around Flora Reef that are coloured with beautiful corals and patrolled by pelagic fish and sharks.

Flinders Reef is a large reef system 200km east of Townsville. Covering an area of over 600 square kilometres and with a large deep water lagoon at its centre, Flinders Reef has some of the most spectacular dive sites in the Coral Sea. Some of the best diving here is on the lagoon pinnacles, with the best of them known as **Watanabe Bommie**.

This office block size pinnacle rises from 45m to 12m and is a breath-taking dive. As soon as you enter the water you will be surrounded by fish, as the top of Watanabe Bommie is always swarming with schools of barracuda, trevally and surgeonfish. If you can drag yourself away from the fish there are radiant corals hanging off the sides of this bommie and a great assortment of reef fish and invertebrates. Divers will also see grey reef sharks, tuna, mackerel and rainbow runners at this incredible dive site.

For divers with a soft spot for wonderful corals there is a site at Flinders Reef that is covered in the most exquisite corals, simply called **Soft Spot**. The series of pinnacles at this site are covered in the most beautiful soft corals – yellows, reds, purples and oranges. Soft Spot varies in depth from 6m to 40m and is also a good location to see reef fish, sharks and pelagics. Other spectacular pinnacles at Flinders Reef are found at **Anemone City**, **Lonely Eel** and **Three Sisters**.

Flinders Cay is a tiny strip of land where an automatic weather station is located and hundreds of sea birds roost. The diving off the cay is quite magic as you don't have to go any deeper than 15m to explore numerous coral heads. Turtles rest in this area, but divers will also see giant clams, garden eels, stingrays, moray eels, coral trout and a wide variety of small reef fish. Flinders Cay is also a great spot for night diving as numerous invertebrate species emerge after dark, including many shrimps, crabs, nudibranchs and flatworms.

The best wall dive at Flinders Reef is at its south-western tip at a site called **Rock Arch**. The wall here drops into 1km of water and is a good spot to see pelagics, but the best part of this dive is exploring the many caves and swim-throughs at the end of the wall where the lagoon starts. One cave in particular is blocked by one of the largest gorgonians that you will see anywhere, over 4m high. At Rock Arch divers will also see humphead parrotfish, reef sharks, red bass, snappers and a colony of garden eels.

There are a number of small reefs around Flinders Reef, but of these the Boomerang Reefs are the most popular. Off the western side of this reef is a spectacular wall dive known as **China Wall**. This wall is so steep that it undercuts itself, and if you suffer from vertigo then you may find it best not to look down into the black void below. Currents generally wash along this wall, allowing drift dives to be done. Expect to see plenty of grey reef sharks, but also silvertip sharks, turtles, Maori wrasse, mackerel, tuna and giant trevally. China Wall is cut with many caves and gutters, with many of these leading into the shallow lagoon, where you can end the dive admiring the abundant reef fish.

Cod Wall is another wonderful wall dive at Boomerang Reefs, with its best feature being the many caves that cut into the wall. These are decorated with soft corals, sea whips and gorgonians, and home to gropers, squirrelfish and the occasional tawny nurse shark. Shark feeds were at one time regularly conducted on the Boomerang Reefs at sites called Hungry Jacks and Scuba Zoo, but these stopped when Mike Ball Dive Expeditions moved from Townsville to Cairns.

The reefs beyond the ones mentioned above are rarely dived, which is unfortunate as incredible diving awaits any diver that can get to **Herald Surprise**, **Abington Reef**, **Diamond Islet**, **Lihou Reefs**, **Herald Cays**, **Chilcott Islet** and **Willis Islet**. The Northern Coral Sea Reefs are a very special area, and once you have experienced the sensational diving here you will understand why many divers are eager to tick this coral wilderness off their bucket list.

NORTHERN CORAL SEA REEFS DIVE DATA

HOW TO GET THERE – A liveaboard charter boat is the only way to explore the Northern Coral Sea Reefs. Bougainville Reef, Holmes Reef and Flora Reef are often included in an extended trip to Osprey Reef, but Flinders Reef and the Boomerang Reefs are only visited on special expeditions. Charter Boats exploring this area generally depart from Cairns, Lizard Island or Townsville. Cairns Airport is serviced by both domestic and international flights, while Townsville Airport only handles domestic flights.

BEST TIME TO VISIT – These reefs can be dived year round.

VISIBILITY – 30m to 50m.

CURRENTS – Generally mild.

WATER TEMPERTURE – Summer highs of 29°C to winter lows of 24°C.

OPPOSITE: Giant soft corals are a feature of the wonderful Northern Coral Sea Reefs.

PELAGIC ENCOUNTERS

Over 1500 species of fish are found on the Great Barrier Reef that range in size from tiny gobies to giant whale sharks. While the colourful reef fish like anemonefish, angelfish and butterflyfish are delightful to watch as they flit around the corals, the most exciting species a diver will encounter, and the ones that get the heart pumping, are the powerful pelagic fish.

Pelagic fish are the wonderers of the reef, roaming the seas from reef to reef, and with much of the Great Barrier Reef protected from fishing they are more common here than just about anywhere else on the planet. Pelagic fish are often found in places with strong currents, but divers will encounter them cruising walls, circling bommies or just hanging under the dive boat.

The trevallys (also known as jacks) are one of the most abundant pelagic species seen on the reef. Giant trevally (*Caranx ignobilis*), turrum trevally (*Carangoides fulvoguttatus*), bluefin trevally (*Caranx lugubris*) and brassy trevally (*Caranx papuensis*) are all common, but a feature of many dive sites on the Great Barrier Reef are massive schools of bigeye trevally (*Caranx sexfasciatus*). Schools of thousands of these spectacular fish are a breathtaking sight, especially when they engulf you in a whirlpool–like formation.

Other wonderful pelagic species encountered in reef waters are rainbow runners (*Elaegatis hipinnulata*), small–toothed jobfish (*Aphareus furca*), shark mackerel (*Grammatorcynus bicarinatus*), Spanish mackerel (*Scomberomorus commerson*) and dogtooth tuna (*Gymnosarda unicolor*). These streamline fish zoom pass divers as they hunt the reef for smaller baitfish.

A number of species of barracuda are also commonly encountered on the Great Barrier Reef. Great barracuda (*Sphyraena barracuda*) grow to 1.5m long and are always an impressive sight. But being circled by a school of hundreds of metre long pickhandle barracuda (*Sphyraena jello*) or chevron barracuda (*Sphyraena putnamiae*) is always an unforgettable experience, and one that can be experienced at many dive sites in this coral wonderland.

OPPOSITE: Schools of big-eye trevally are common on many dive sites on the Great Barrier Reef.

Eddy Reef

Beaver Reef

Mission Beach

Dunk Island

Otter Reef

Rockingham Bay

Lady Bowen

Britomart Reef

Hinchinbrook Island

Trunk Reef

0   10   20 km
0   5   10 n mile

MISSION BEACH

Located halfway between Cairns and Townsville, Mission Beach is a popular holiday town for people looking for pretty beaches to sunbake, lush rainforest to explore or just a quiet place for a relaxing getaway. This part of Queensland is called the Cassowary Coast, as a number of these giant flightless rainforest birds are native to the area, but for divers the main attraction at Mission Beach is a brilliant shipwreck called the **Lady Bowen**.

Only rediscovered in 1996, the *Lady Bowen* is an impressive shipwreck that put Mission Beach on the diving map, especially after reports that it was covered in marine life almost as prolific as the famous SS *Yongala*. But the wreck of the *Lady Bowen* isn't the only dive attraction in the area as offshore from Mission Beach are numerous reefs, and a few other wrecks, that provide wonderful diving.

The *Lady Bowen* was a four mast schooner, built in Glasgow in 1864. On the 19th August 1894, the 75m long iron hull ship was sailing down the Queensland coast when it ran aground on Kennedy Shoal, 35km southeast of Mission Beach. The ship drifted off the shoal but started to breakup, so the crew took to the lifeboats and abandoned the stricken vessel. The crew safely made it ashore, but the *Lady Bowen* disappeared below the waves and wasn't seen again for over 100 years.

Today the *Lady Bowen* is an incredible dive, but resting at a depth of 33m, and often washed by strong currents, it is a dive for advanced divers only. The ship rests upright on the bottom and is basically an open hull waiting to be explored. The skeletal ribs of the ship are fascinating to investigate, but parts of the decking remain, forming a cave like structure for fish to shelter under. The bow is the most prominent part of the ship, rising 6m off the bottom and capped with a T shaped cross beam. Other features of this interesting shipwreck are the smoke stack, the anchor winch and the stern structure.

OPPOSITE: A common species seen on the reefs off Mission Beach is the pink anemonefish.

113

While the wreck itself is captivating to explore the best feature of the *Lady Bowen* is its resident marine life. Schooling fish swarm on and above the shipwreck; snappers, trevally, barracuda, batfish, emperors, sweetlips, fusiliers and clouds of baitfish. Other common fish species encountered are pufferfish, coral trout, lionfish, surgeonfish, angelfish, coral cod and numerous gropers.

The wreck is also home to stingrays, eagle rays, reef sharks and turtles, but divers have also spotted leopard sharks and white-spotted shovel rays resting on the sand beside the wreck. The *Lady Bowen* is particularly infested with olive sea snakes, with dozens seen on a typical dive. The wreck is also very colourful, with sea whips, gorgonians, sponges and tubastra corals decorating the hull. The *Lady Bowen* is one special dive, but divers need to be watchful of their bottom time as it is easy to get distracted watching the parade of marine life on this magnificent shipwreck.

There are numerous reefs off Mission Beach and most are largely unexplored, but several of the inner reefs are visited by day boats and offer wonderful diving. Eddy Reef is a small reef system northeast of Mission Beach that has rich coral gardens. The most popular dive site here is on the southern side and is simply called **Eddy**. This cove in the reef varies in depth from 6m to 20m and offers the diver a little bit of everything; walls, gutters, ledges and pretty corals. Expect to see coral trout, batfish, angelfish, sweetlips, barramundi cod, snappers, surgeonfish and a good assortment of invertebrate species.

Beaver Reef is another popular destination off Mission Beach which has a number of brilliant dive sites. **Beavers Cay**, located on the northern side of the reef, has gorgeous coral formations in depths from 12m to 22m, where divers will find turtles, stingrays, fusiliers, trevally and reef sharks. But this site is best over the winter months when manta rays cruise the area. Off the southern side of Beaver Reef is another brilliant site called **Shark Alley**. This dive site features a sloping coral wall that drops into 15m and is a great place to encounter whitetip reef sharks and blacktip reef sharks.

Otter Reef is the largest reef system in the area and has some of the best dive sites off Mission Beach. **North Wall** is a spectacular large bommie that plummets

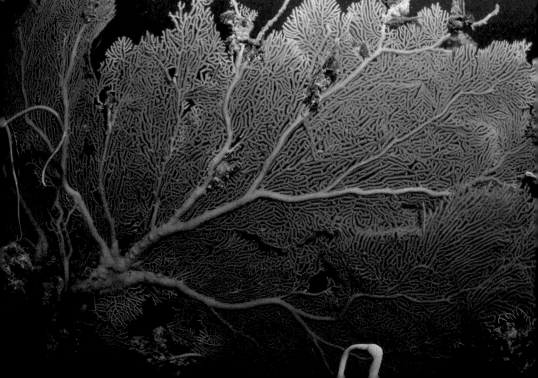

from the surface to 25m. Currents often wash this bommie and ensure that its walls are covered in spectacular soft corals and gorgonians. While nudibranchs and other small critters can be seen here, divers will be most impressed by the larger pelagics like trevally, barracuda, batfish and mackerel. **South Wall** is a similar large bommie on the southern side of Otter Reef, where divers will encounter reef sharks, stingrays and turtles. But for an exciting drift dive head to **Trevally Pass**, and zoom along a reef wall with the trevally, fusiliers and snappers.

There are many other wonderful reef dive sites off Mission Beach, and also a few more wrecks. Two World War II plane wrecks are found in murky inshore waters, so are rarely dived, but for those into tek diving there are a number of shipwrecks in deeper, clear water that are awaiting exploration off Mission Beach.

MISSION BEACH DIVE DATA

HOW TO GET THERE – Mission Beach is located hallway between Cairns and Townsville, with regular bus services from both cities. Day boats visit the local dive sites, but occasionally liveaboard vessels stop off at the *Lady Bowen* shipwreck.

BEST TIME TO VISIT – Year round.

VISIBILITY – 15m to 30m, with the clearest water on the outer reefs.

CURRENTS – Generally only mild currents, but strong currents can be experienced on the *Lady Bowen* shipwreck.

WATER TEMPERTURE – Summer highs of 29°C to winter lows of 24°C.

OPPOSITE TOP: Part of the bow structure of the impressive shipwreck, the *Lady Bowen*.

OPPOSITE BOTTOM: Divers will find the reefs off Mission Beach are richly decorated with beautiful corals, including large gorgonians.

— FEATURE —
REEF CRITTERS

While most visitors come to the Great Barrier Reef to see the lovely corals and the reef's larger residents like sharks, turtles, rays and fish, the reef is alive with many smaller fascinating critters, you just have to be prepared to look.

Nudibranchs are one of the most beautiful and colourful creatures a diver will find on the Great Barrier Reef. Many species of these colourful sea slugs are found in the area, but most don't sit out in the open, so divers have to look under ledges, in caves and on reef walls to spot these pretty critters. The easiest way to find most nudibranchs is to locate their food source, such as sponges, bryozoans and ascidians, as they are never too far away.

Many shrimp species live on the Great Barrier Reef, but as they are small, and some even have transparent bodies, they can be easily overlooked. The banded boxer shrimp (*Stenopus hispidus*) is the most common shrimp on the reef and are usually found in holes or under corals. Many commensal shrimp species are also quite common and a good place to find them is living in anemones. While most shrimps only emerge at night, you may be lucky enough to see a colourful peacock mantis shrimp (*Odontodactylus scyllarus*) scuttling across the bottom during the day looking for food or a new home.

Octopus are amazing creatures that can change their shape, colour and general appearance in the blink of an eye. Several species are seen on the Great Barrier Reef, but are often overlooked because of their exceptional camouflage. Some octopus like to hide amongst the coral, others in holes in the reef, while a few live in the sand. While more common at night, octopus are often observed sneaking across the coral to avoid being harassed by fish or when pursing a mate.

OPPOSITE TOP: Many colourful nudibranch species are found in reef waters.

OPPOSITE BOTTOM: The day octopus is often encountered by divers on the Great Barrier Reef.

Hinchinbrook Island

Trunk Reef

Myrmidon Reef

Roxburgh Reef

Pelorus Island

Orpheus Island

Ingham

Great Palm Island

Lodestone Reef

Chicken Reef

Keeper Reef

Anzac Reefs

Wheeler Reef

Broadhurst Reef

Magnetic Island

Townsville

SS Yongala

Old Reef

0   10   20 km

0   5   10 n mile

TOWNSVILLE

Most divers travel to Townsville to explore just one dive site, the legendary shipwreck – the SS *Yongala*. This shipwreck is such an incredible dive that it deserves a chapter of its own, but divers shouldn't be mistaken into thinking that this is the only amazing dive site off Townsville.

Townsville is the capital of north Queensland and while not as tourist driven as Cairns, it is still a great place to holiday and has many attractions. For those into shipwrecks, especially if diving the SS *Yongala,* a visit to the Maritime Museum of Townsville is not to be missed as it has many artefacts from the historic shipwreck. While the Museum of Tropical Queensland contains the best collection of maritime relics in the state, including items recovered from HMS *Pandora*. A visit to Magnetic Island is also highly recommended as you can swim, snorkel and bushwalk, and enjoy close encounters with wild wallabies and koalas. And for those that want to see the best of the Great Barrier Reef, without getting wet, there is the Reef HQ Aquarium, with displays of many typical reef species.

For those that prefer to get wet and explore the reef for themselves there are a great collection of coral reefs off Townsville that are accessible on either day boats or liveaboards. There are actually so many reefs off Townsville that some only have numbers and many are still waiting to be explored.

Mrymidon Reef is an isolated outpost beyond the main reef system that offers outstanding diving. All around this reef are steep and sloping walls that drop into depths of 30m and more. Many of these walls are deeply cut by enormous caves that will keep you entertained for an entire dive. Expect to find coral trout, Maori wrasse, gropers, squirrelfish and some beautiful gorgonians in these caves. While cruising the walls are mackerel, trevally, reef sharks and the occasional spotted eagle ray.

OPPOSITE: A school of gold-lined rabbitfish hover over a bommie at Keeper Reef.

On other parts of Mrymidon Reef the walls are cut by deep gutters that are decorated with hard corals, soft corals, sponges and sea whips. Some of these gutters lead into shallow water where lovely hard coral gardens flourish. Abundant reef fish, reef sharks, turtles and some of the biggest giant clams you will ever see populate these coral gardens. Early morning is one of the best times to explore these coral gardens as herds of humphead parrotfish swim through to graze on the corals.

Lodestone Reef is a popular destination for day trips and has a number of dive sites that offer wonderful diving. In the shallows are coral gardens and canyons which are a good place to see colourful reef fish and invertebrate species, such as angelfish, blue tangs, rock cods, sea stars, anemonefish and nudibranchs. While beyond 20m are bommies decorated with soft corals and gorgonians that are visited by trevally, barracuda, reef sharks and turtles.

The western side of **Keeper Reef** is a maze of bommies, gutters and coral ridges in depths from 8m to 20m. It is easy to get lost in this complex of coral, as much of the coral looks the same, but divers also get distracted looking at all the fish. Massive schools of fusiliers cover the reef, but divers will also see numerous species of angelfish, triggerfish, sweetlips, snappers and lionfish. Larger residents include green turtles, coral trout, whitetip reef sharks and barramundi cod.

Wheeler Reef is a small reef with a lot to offer. The fish life at this site is always brilliant, especially off the western side of the reef where numerous bommies rise from 30m. A resident school of barracuda is always seen here, and they seem to delight in circling divers. Also common are schools of trevally, fusiliers and rabbitfish, but divers will likely encounter Maori wrasse, coral trout, sweetlips and turtles. In the shallows at Wheeler Reef are many sandy patches where stingrays and garden eels can be seen. The corals at Wheeler Reef are also very beautiful, with spectacular gorgonians and soft corals in deeper water and a great collection of hard corals in the shallows.

Divers will find a great deal of interesting terrain to explore at **Chicken Reef**. Walls, bommies, gutters and caves are just some of the features of this reef in depths from 10m to 30m. On deeper parts of the reef are beautiful gorgonians and forests of sea whips, and a close look at these corals will reveal sea whip gobies and allied cowries. Potato cod, moray eels, whitetip reef sharks,

OPPOSITE TOP: Wheeler Reef is a great place to find lovely gorgonian fans.

OPPOSITE BOTTOM: The biggest set of lips on the reef belong to the many-spotted sweetlips.

OVERLEAF, CLOCKWISE FROM TOP LEFT: Painted crayfish shelter under ledges and in caves throughout the Great Barrier Reef; with so many fish species on the Great Barrier Reef, many smaller species like this eastern triplefin are often overlooked; the gold-spotted nudibranch is a common species on the reefs off Townsville; adding a splash of colour to any reef is the lovely Hefferman's seastar.

humphead parrotfish, Maori wrasse and schools of snapper are a few of the species seen at Chicken Reef.

Anzac Reef has a number of interesting dive sites, but its best is a giant pinnacle called **Anzac Bommie**. This wonderful tower of coral rises from 35m and is always covered in fish life. Schools of snapper, goatfish, trevally and barracuda are common, but divers will also encounter turtles, grey reef sharks, gropers and coral trout. The best way to explore Anzac Bommie is to start in deep water and slowly swim circuits around the pinnacle, gradually rising into shallow water. Down deeper are the most colourful corals; the gorgonians, black coral trees, spikey soft corals and sponges. Numerous crevasses cut into the bommie and are a home to coral cod, squirrelfish, moray eels, hawkfish and nudibranchs. At night Anzac Bommie is a mesmerising sight, with the corals much more radiant under torch light. After dark crustaceans emerge from every nook and cranny, parrotfish can be found tucked up in holes and octopus stalk the reef look to make a meal out of an unsuspecting crab. But a highlight are the many basketstars that perch on the reef and fan out their metre wide arms to capture food particles.

Broadhurst Reef is one of the largest reef systems off Townsville and has an extensive lagoon, plus walls and bommies to explore. Most dives here are in depths

ABOVE: Healthy gardens of hard coral are a feature of the reefs off Townsville.

126

between 12m and 25m, but some of the walls drop into much deeper water. Pelagic action is usually best off the walls, especially if a gentle current is running, as divers are likely to see mackerel, dogtooth tuna, barracuda, rainbow runners and maybe the occasional eagle ray or mobula ray. Also common at Broadhurst Reef are whitetip reef sharks, turtles, stingrays and schools of sweetlips.

The SS *Yongala* is not the only shipwreck that can be dived off Townsville as another historic shipwreck is found at Old Reef. The **SS Gottenburg** was a 60m long steam ship, built in London in 1854. While on a voyage from Darwin to Adelaide the ship was driven onto Old Reef on 24 February 1875 after being caught in a fierce cyclone. The ship soon became a total wreck and over one hundred people were lost in the horrendous conditions.

Today the SS *Gottenburg* is very broken up, spread across the western side of the reef in depths from 9m to 16m. The boiler is the most distinctive feature, but divers can also see davits, bollards, engine components and twisted plates and ribs. Numerous fish shelter amongst the wreckage with coral trout, gropers, snappers, blacktip reef sharks and fusiliers common.

There are many other reefs off Townsville, but most of these are not visited by charter boats. Divers and snorkelers can also explore a number of continental islands that are closer to Townsville. Day trips to **Pelorus Island** and **Orpheus Island** are popular, and the coral gardens around these islands are surprisingly good. **Magnetic Island** is also a wonderful place to snorkel and dive, and even has a number of shore diving options. The best of these is the *Moltke* shipwreck, which is found in Geoffrey Bay and covered in corals and reef fish.

If you travel all the way to Townsville to dive the SS *Yongala,* ensure you leave a few days up your sleeve to also explore some of the wonderful reefs and islands in the area.

TOWNSVILLE DIVE DATA

HOW TO GET THERE – Townsville Airport is regularly serviced by domestic flights from across Australia. Divers have to choice of day trips to the reef or islands, or a liveaboard trip, which generally includes a visit to the SS *Yongala.*

BEST TIME TO VISIT – Year round.

VISIBILITY – 6m to 10m around the islands, but 20m to 30m on the offshore reefs.

CURRENTS – mild on most reefs in the area.

WATER TEMPERTURE – Summer highs of 28°C to winter lows of 23°C.

– FEATURE –
CORAL SPAWNING

One of the most amazing natural wonders of the world was discovered by scientists on the Great Barrier Reef in 1981, the annual coral spawning.

Most corals are hermaphrodites, having both male and female reproductive cells, and reproduce in a number of different ways. Corals can simply clone themselves, through several forms of asexual reproduction, but spawning is the most common form of reproduction and the most spectacular.

The corals of the Great Barrier Reef spawn at the start of summer, just after the full moon in either October, November or December. Three factors have been found to trigger the mass spawning; rising water temperatures, the lunar cycle and the diurnal cycle (night time).

When the time if right, four to five nights after the full moon (when water movements are at a minimum), coral species across the reef release their eggs and sperm into the water column simultaneously. The eggs are tiny pink balls, while the sperm is a milky cloud, and together they turn the surface of the sea into a thick pink soup, called a spawn slick.

Once an egg is fertilised an embryo develops within 24 hours, known as a planula. After drifting with the currents for around five days the tiny embryo settles on the bottom and start to grow into a new coral colony.

Numerous fish species, manta rays and even whale sharks feed on this coral spawn, and while billions of eggs get eaten by predators, billions more survive to settle on the bottom and ensure a new generation of corals appear.

Timing a visit to witness the annual coral spawn is a tricky proposition, as predicting the month and time of the event on different parts of the reef is difficult. While the spawning can last up to a week, it generally happens at different times on the inner and outer reefs. Generally the inner reefs are the first to spawn in October, while the outer reefs follow in either November or December.

The annual coral spawning on the Great Barrier Reef is a spectacular event, but you may have to suffer many sleepless nights to witness it.

OPPOSITE: One of the most spectacular events a diver can witness on the Great Barrier Reef is the annual coral spawning (image by Darren Jew).

SS YONGALA

The SS *Yongala* is regularly listed in the top ten dive sites in the world, and for a very good reason. This incredible shipwreck, located south of Townsville, is buzzing with more marine life than you will see at any other dive site on the planet.

Built in England in 1903, the SS *Yongala* was a steel passenger and cargo steam ship owned by the Adelaide Steamship Company. Named after a town in South Australia, the ship was 109m long, weighed 3664 tons and had a top speed of 15.8 knots. After arriving in Australia, the SS *Yongala* first went into service carrying passengers and freight between Western Australia and the eastern states. But later switched to the Melbourne to Cairns route.

On her 99th voyage the SS *Yongala* departed Melbourne on the 14th of March 1911, under the command of Captain William Knight. After calling in at Brisbane and Mackay, the ship headed north, right into the path of a cyclone. The ship was never seen again. On board the ship were 50 passengers and 73 crew; all were lost on the night of March 23 when the ship tragically sank.

While some cargo and the body of a racehorse washed ashore, no trace of the ship was found at the time. But years later, sightings of a ghost ship, fitting the description of the SS *Yongala*, were reported off the coast of Townsville from time to time.

Then in 1943 a minesweeper located a large submerged object in the shipping channel 12 nautical miles east of Cape Bowling Green. It was thought to be a shipwreck, but wasn't confirmed as the SS *Yongala* until divers visited the site in 1958.

Today the SS *Yongala* rests on its starboard side in depths from 15m to 29m. Protected as a historic shipwreck in 1981, no artefacts can be removed from the wreck site. Divers are also prohibited from penetrating the ship to help preserve the steel structure. But divers don't need to enter the SS *Yongala* to have a brilliant dive.

OPPOSITE: A diver explores the bow of the historic shipwreck SS *Yongala*.

While many of the ship's features are plain to see, such as the rudder, engines, masts, portholes, bollards, lifeboat davits and even the toilets, the main reason divers explore the shipwreck is not to see rusting metal, but marine life, and plenty of it.

Sitting on the sea floor and being the only shelter in a vast plain of sand the shipwreck is an oasis for marine life, attracting an astonishing variety of species. Vast schools of fish engulf the shipwreck, with millions of cardinalfish, baitfish and damselfish providing a feast for turrum trevally, Spanish mackerel, bonito, queenfish, wahoo and other pelagic species.

Under the stern is usually a thick school of painted sweetlips, while massive schools of stripy snapper, black-spot snapper, one-spot snapper and five-lined snapper mill around the masts and engine room area. The water column above the wreck is always swirling with fish, with immense schools of barracuda, batfish and giant trevally seen.

Some of the resident reef fish includes coral trout, Maori wrasse, mangrove jacks, red emperors, tuskfish, parrotfish, angelfish, moray eels, lionfish, butterfly-fish, pufferfish, coral cod and surgeonfish. The groper family is particularly well represented on the SS *Yongala*, with flowery gropers, estuary gropers and a number of huge Queensland gropers seen on every dive.

Dozens of turtles call the wreck home and can be seen sleeping, feeding or heading to the surface to get fresh air. Two species of sea snake also reside on the wreck, but are so accustomed to divers that they generally ignore the bubble-blowing aliens invading their realm.

The most common ray species seen on the wreck are spotted eagle rays and black-blotched stingrays. Both species like to hover on top of the wreck, especially if a current is running. Other ray species seen here include white-spotted shovelnose rays, pink stingrays, estuary stingrays, cowtail stingrays, leopard whiprays and even the odd manta ray or shark ray.

Shark encounters on the SS *Yongala* are almost guaranteed with tawny nurse sharks and tasselled wobbegong sharks found resting under wreckage. Plus blacktip sharks and bull sharks are often seen patrolling the waters around the wreck. But divers have also seen leopard sharks, whale sharks and even the occasional tiger shark.

Another feature of the SS *Yongala* is the wonderful corals that decorate the hull. Almost every part of the ship is covered by the most exquisite corals – forests of sea whips, lovely black coral trees, radiant spikey soft corals and delicate

OPPOSITE TOP: The fish life on the SS *Yongala* is unbelievable, and constantly swirling around the wreck.

OPPOSITE BOTTOM: A diver swims along the wreck of the SS *Yongala*.

ABOVE: Olive sea snakes are a common dive companion on the SS *Yongala*.

OPPOSITE TOP: Corals and fish completely cover the SS *Yongala*, and are so dense they obscure the wreck.

OPPOSITE BOTTOM: Strange bed fellows, a tawny nurse shark and a loggerhead turtle found sleeping under the SS *Yongala*.

candelabra gorgonians have transformed the rust into a tapestry of colour. And there is no shortage of invertebrate species, but these are rarely noticed as most divers can't take their eyes off all the fish.

One word of warning, the SS *Yongala* might be one of the best dive sites in the world, but it doesn't always have the best visibility. But you don't need great visibility to enjoy the wreck as the fish and other marine life will leave your head spinning no matter how clear it is.

Allow at least a week to fully appreciate all the marine life this special shipwreck has to offer, as it changes hour by hour and day by day. The SS *Yongala* is a dive site you will never forget.

SS *YONGALA* DIVE DATA

HOW TO GET THERE – The SS *Yongala* is accessible via day boats departing from Townsville and Alva Beach (near Ayr), and on liveaboard trips departing from Townsville. Townsville Airport is regularly serviced by domestic flights from across Australia.

BEST TIME TO VISIT – Year round.

VISIBILITY – 6m to 10m on average, but up to 30m at times.

CURRENTS – Very common and very strong at times.

WATER TEMPERTURE – Summer highs of 28°C to winter lows of 23°C.

– FEATURE –
GIANTS OF THE WRECK

The largest fish divers will encounter on the SS *Yongala* is the unforgettable Queensland groper (*Epinephelus lanceolatus*). Also known as the giant groper, these massive fish reach a length of 3m and can weigh up to 400kg. Found throughout the Indo–Pacific region, Queensland gropers feed on almost anything they can grab; other fish, small sharks, sea snakes and even juvenile turtles.

It is not known how many of these huge fish reside on the SS *Yongala*, but on most dives two or three are encountered, and all are massive, well over 2m long. These gropers are accustomed to divers exploring their home, but they still don't like people getting too close. As they swim around the wreck they are usually accompanied by an entourage of small fish, with remoras stuck to them, golden trevally guiding them and a cloud of oxeye scad swarming around them. These giant fish are another reason why the SS *Yongala* is such an incredible dive site.

Jacqueline Reef

Kangaroo Reef (East)

Ellen Reef

Elizabeth Reef

Eulalie I

Wallaby Reef

Cobham Reef

Kennedy Reef

Gould Reef

Showers Reef

Net Reef

Knuckle
Reef

Martin Reef

Fairey Reef (No 1)

Seagull
Reef

Fairey Reef (No 2)

Fairey Reef (No 3)

Outlier Reef

Line Reef

Sinker Reef

Block Reef

Hardy Reef

Bait Reef

Hook Reef

Dolphin Point

Hayman Island

Pinnacle Point

Langford Island

Bird Island

Hook
Island

Black Island

Daydream Island

Airlie Beach

Whitsunday
Island

Hamilton Island

Long Island

Shaw Island

0		10		20 km
0	5		10 n mile	

WHITSUNDAYS

M any visitors to the Whitsunday Islands journey to this region to relax at an exclusive resort, sail around the pretty islands or to explore the many national parks in the area. But these continental islands are fringed by coral reefs that offer delightful snorkelling and diving opportunities, and not far offshore are a number of wonderful coral reefs.

The 74 heavily wooded islands of the Whitsunday Group are located off the popular holiday town of Airlie Beach. Several of the islands have world class resorts, such as Hayman Island, Hamilton Island, Daydream Island and Long Island, but most of the Whitsunday Islands are uninhabited and national parks.

Several of the resorts have dive operations and offer day trips around the islands and to the reef. Day boats to the reef also operate from Airlie Beach. However, one of the best ways to explore this area is on a liveaboard vessel and in the Whitsundays they do this sort of trip slightly different. These liveaboard trips are generally only two to three days long and are a combination of diving, sailing and exploring the islands. A Whitsunday liveaboard trip is generally not suited to the hardcore diver that wants to do five dives a day, but perfect if you have a non-diving partner or if you like to take your diving a little easy. Some of these trips only travel around the islands, but the best combine a trip around the islands with a day or two on the nearby coral reefs.

At the northern end of Hayman Island is one of the most popular dive sites in the Whitsunday Islands, **Blue Pearl Bay**. The rocky gutters, ridges and ledges at this site vary in depth from 5m to 20m and are completely covered in the most beautiful corals – hard corals, soft corals and small gorgonians. Blue Pearl Bay is a great location for macro photography as nudibranchs, flatworms, shrimps, crabs, sea stars, anemones and small reef fish are common. But divers will find no shortage of larger fish at this site with sweetlips, angelfish, snappers, coral trout, trevally and several large Maori wrasse to be seen. At the northern end of this bay is a spot called **Dolphin Point** that is exposed to more currents, but divers are more likely to see pelagic fish and reef sharks here.

Some of the best dive sites in the Whitsunday area are located at the northern end of Hook Island. **Manta Ray Bay** and **Luncheon Bay** are right next to each other and have much the same terrain and marine life. Pick a depth to suit your experience as the rocky terrain here is covered in corals in depths from 1m to 20m. Divers will find gutters, caves and ledges to explore that are coloured with radiant soft corals. Reef fish and invertebrate species are found in abundance, but so are sweetlips, coral trout, batfish, moray eels, trevally and Maori wrasse. Whitetip reef sharks, blue spotted stingrays and large Spanish mackerel frequent this area, but don't forget to look up every now and then as manta rays cruise this area, especially over the winter months.

If conditions are right, and light southerly winds are blowing, a visit to Hook Island's most spectacular dive site might be on the cards, the wonderful **Pinnacle Point**. This site features numerous bommies and caves in depths from 3m to 22m, but is often washed by strong currents. The corals at this site are just lovely, but Pinnacle Point is a great spot to see big fish – barracuda, trevally, mackerel, coral trout, Maori wrasse, sweetlips, gropers and batfish. Whitetip and blacktip reef sharks are often encountered in this area, and manta rays are known to make a guest appearance.

There are many other dive sites around Hook Island and in this general area of the Whitsunday Islands, including Bird Island, Black Island and Langford Reef. But most of these sites are rarely visited by charter boats.

Most reef diving off the Whitsundays is done on a group of inner reefs 50km east of Airlie Beach. Fairey Reef is the most northern of these reefs and has a number of brilliant dive sites awaiting exploration. **Henry's Bommie** is on the northwest side of the reef and going no deeper than 15m divers can explore a pretty bommie, coral gutters or several small caves. A good collection of reef fish reside here, but divers will also see giant clams, moray eels and turtles.

Off the western side of the reef is **Little Fairey Inlet**, where a nice coral wall drops to 16m. The corals along this wall are dominated by hard and soft corals, but a few lovely gorgonians can also be viewed. Swimming along the wall divers will see sweetlips, angelfish, parrotfish, butterflyfish and a number of nudibranchs.

Hardy Reef is the location of the **Reefworld Pontoon**, which is visited by day boats from Airlie Beach. The diving around the pontoon is quite nice, with

OPPOSITE TOP: The bold pattern of the clown triggerfish makes it a popular subject for underwater photographers.

OPPOSITE BOTTOM: Giant Maori wrasse are seen at dive sites throughout the Great Barrier Reef, with a number seen at Bait Reef.

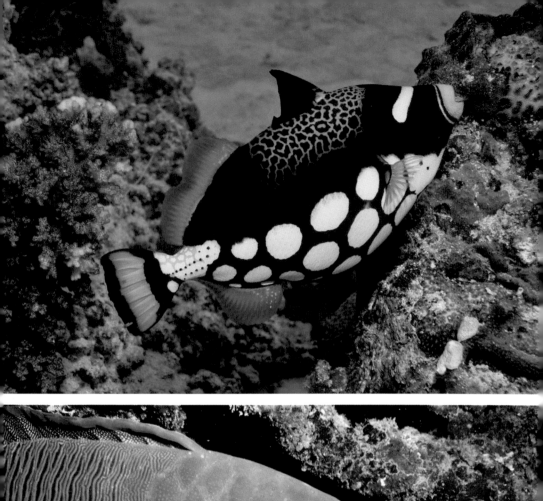

coral gardens and a reef sloping into 18m. But the main feature is all the very tame fish that congregate under the pontoon. Having been hand fed, the fish are in-your-mask all the time and include gropers, sweetlips, trevally, damsels, fusiliers, snappers and Maori wrasse.

Wonderful reef diving is also found at Hook Reef, Line Reef, Sinker Reef and Black Reef, but Bait Reef is the most popular location for both day boats and liveaboard boats. Bait Reef is only small, but it has a sheltered lagoon and several excellent dive sites that both divers and snorkelers will enjoy.

Stepping Stones is located off the western side of Bait Reef and is a collection of 18 large bommies that look like giant stepping stones from the air. This string of bommies covers such a wide area that it would take over a dozen dives to explore the entire site. The bommies rise from depths between 15m and 25m and terminate just below the surface. The best corals are found beyond 20m, where large gorgonians and soft corals sprout from the bottom. But many divers never get this deep as the gutters and large caves found between each bommie provide a lot of entertainment.

Marine life around the Stepping Stones is quite prolific; out deeper pelagic fish and reef sharks are common, while between the bommies are schools of sweetlips, fusiliers and snapper. Divers will also see coral trout, flowery gropers, barramundi cod, moray eels and a number of large Maori wrasse. The shallow side of the bommies is populated with a good variety of reef fish and invertebrates that will keep any photographer happy. At the end of your dive you can also follow one of the many gutters into the lagoon where fields of staghorn coral cover the bottom. Stingrays, turtles and small reef sharks are often found in this area.

At the very end of the Stepping Stones is a site called **Hawaii**. The bommies here rise from deeper water and this is generally the best place to see pelagic action and sharks. Common here are schools of trevally, mackerel, batfish, barracuda and a few grey reef sharks.

The best dive site at Bait Reef is found off its southern side and is known as **Manta Ray Drop Off**. This wall varies greatly along its length and it takes a few dives to explore. Parts of the wall drop from the surface straight to 75m, while in other sections it slopes to 20m and then drops. But anywhere you dive here you will see a parade of passing pelagic fish. Gangs of Spanish mackerel, trevally and bonito attack smaller fish, especially if schools of baitfish are present. But also cruising this wall are batfish, barracuda and a surprising number of turtles.

OPPOSITE TOP: The largest stingray species divers will encounter on the Great Barrier Reef is the impressive black blotched stingray.

OPPOSITE BOTTOM: Numerous green turtles are seen drifting along the wall at Manta Ray Drop Off.

Many caves and ledges cut into the wall and these accommodate coral trout, gropers, sweetlips, squirrelfish, snappers and surgeonfish. Whitetip reef sharks, grey reef sharks and silvertip sharks also patrol the wall at Manta Ray Drop Off, as do manta rays, but they are more commonly seen over the winter months.

The Whitsunday region may not have the clearest waters of the Great Barrier Reef, but it certainly has a great variety of marine life and dive sites that any diver will enjoy.

WHITSUNDAY DIVE DATA

HOW TO GET THERE – The Whitsunday region is serviced by two airports, at Proserpine and on Hamilton Island. Day boats depart from Airlie Beach (or nearby Shute Harbour) and from a few of the resort islands. Liveaboard boats usually depart from Airlie Beach.

BEST TIME TO VISIT – The Whitsunday region can be dived year round, but the water around the islands is often clearest over the winter months.

VISIBILITY – Around the islands the visibility varies from 3m to 15m, while on the reef 12m to 25m.

CURRENTS – Mild to strong currents are common around the islands, as this area has quite a large tidal range. Mild currents are typical on the reef.

WATER TEMPERTURE – Summer highs of 28°C to winter lows of 22°C.

ABOVE: Divers can often get very close to the green turtles at Bait Reef.

OPPOSITE: Beautiful coral gardens are found at the dive sites around Hook Island.

MERMAID OF THE REEF

A number of whale and dolphin species are found on the Great Barrier Reef, but another much rarer and unusual marine mammal is also found in this area, the dugong (*Dugong dugon*).

Believed to be the source of sailor's tales of mermaids, dugongs are herbivorous mammals found in the tropical waters of the Indo-Pacific region. Reaching a length of 3m and weighing up to 400kg, dugongs feed almost exclusively on seagrasses, and consume up to 40kg a day to maintain their trim figure. They are generally found in the inshore waters of the Great Barrier Reef,

where seagrass meadows flourish in shallow bays, and are often seen around the Whitsunday Islands.

Dugongs live up to 70 years, but have a low reproduction rate, only producing a calf every four to five years. Listed as vulnerable across their range, the dugong population in northern Australia, at around 80,000, is the largest and most important in the world. But even in Australia dugongs face pressures from habitat loss, boat strikes and entanglement in fishing nets.

Underwater encounters with dugongs are extremely rare, and you are far more likely to see them from the surface. These shy animals are usually wary of divers, but every now and then a curious individual will investigate a diver for an unforgettable encounter with a mermaid.

Neville Coleman Reef
(Blue Hole)

Zodiac Cay   Distant Cay

                    Riptide Cay   Lavers Cay

Mullers Reef   Centenery Cay
Storm Cay   Perfect Lagoon Reef

                              Mystery Cay

Heralds Reef Prong   East Cay

Heralds Prong No 2   Thomas Cay

                                              Central Reef

                              Gannet Cay
                                        Horseshoe Reef
        Snake Reef   Sanctuary Reef

            Herald No 1   Hook Reef
                                              Sinker Reef
                                        Sandshoe Reef

                        Hackie Reef   Sweetlip Ree

                                        Hixson Cay

0   20 km
0   10 n mile

SWAIN REEFS

The Great Barrier Reef hugs the Queensland coastline as it journeys south, never more than 50km offshore. But at its southern end it kicks out wide of the coast to form a complex labyrinth known as the Swain Reefs.

The Swain Reefs are an incredible group of reefs, 100km to 200km off the mainland, northeast of the port of Gladstone. A major hazard for ships, the Swain Reefs have claimed numerous vessels over the years and most ships give this area a very wide berth. The reefs in this area are so tightly packed together that strong currents are common, and in some spots the water between reefs is more like a running river with whirlpools and standing waves creating a hazard for boats. But these strong currents also bring a wealth of nutrients, making the Swain Reefs one of the richest areas of the Great Barrier Reef.

More famous as a fishing destination, as only a small proportion of the reefs are protected as green zones, the Swain Reefs offer the diver outstanding diving on bommies, walls and wonderful coral gardens. While some of the larger table fish, such as coral trout and sweetlips, may be harder to find on the reefs where fishing is allowed, divers will still see a great abundance of marine life, including sea snakes, reef sharks, stingrays, turtles and pelagic fish. Being so far offshore a liveaboard vessel is the only way to dive the Swain Reefs, but unfortunately trips to this area are sadly few and far between. However, if you can get to the Swain Reefs you will find many wonderful established dive sites and many reefs that have never been explored.

At the northern end of the Swain Reefs is a wonderful dive site called **Riptide Cay**, and it certainly lives up to its name as the currents rip around this small reef. But between tides the waters are calm enough for divers to explore the lovely coral gardens and small bommies off the northern end of

OPPOSITE: Many rock cod species are found on the Great Barrier Reef, including the attractive small-toothed rock cod.

the reef. Because of the currents the corals are lush and healthy, and the fish life very abundant. Schools of trevally, rainbow runners, snappers and parrotfish are common, but divers should also watch out for sweetlips, rabbitfish, red emperors, coral trout, mackerel and a surprising number of blue spotted lagoon rays. Amongst the corals shelter a good variety of invertebrate species, including nudibranchs, sea stars, crayfish and numerous giant clams.

One of the best dive sites at **Lavers Cay** is a series of impressive coral canyons on the northeast side of the reef. These canyons are found in depths between 12m and 22m and are covered in pretty hard and soft corals. A family of giant Queensland gropers call this site home, and these 2m long fish are very curious of visiting divers. Lavers Cay is also a good spot to see giant trevally, whitetip reef sharks, batfish, coral trout, bonito, sweetlips and a good variety of angelfish.

The coral gardens on the northern side of **Perfect Lagoon Reef** are a great place to find olive sea snakes. Around a dozen of these marine reptiles can be seen on most dives, slowly cruising around the corals looking for potential prey. Forests of staghorn corals decorate this site in depths to 20m and provide a shelter for numerous reef fish and invertebrate species.

Mystery Cay has a number of great dive sites and is the best place in the Swain Reefs to see manta rays. These giant rays glide around the reef and visit the many cleaning stations in the area. The diving off the western side of the reef is very enjoyable as the extensive coral gardens here are divided by countless gutters in only 15m of water. This reef is richly populated with reef and pelagic fish, including trevally, Maori wrasse, sweetlips, emperors and rabbitfish. Olive sea snakes are constant dive companions, but are best ignored if they make you nervous. Whitetip reef sharks and tawny nurse sharks are often seen in this area, but make sure you take a close look at the coral rubble in the gutters as mantis shrimps and spider shells are found in this zone.

Mystery Cay also has a large lagoon and is a great location for night diving. Many small bommies dot the sandy lagoon in depths to 10m, and under torch light divers will find coral crabs, shrimps, hermit crabs, decorator crabs, nudibranchs, flatworms and squid. Many shells also emerge from the sand after dark so keep an eye out for volutes, cones and other pretty species.

OPPOSITE TOP: Hermit crabs have a soft abdomen and to protect their soft underbelly they use old shells as mobile homes.

OPPOSITE BOTTOM: The banded boxer shrimp is a very common reef species that shelter under ledges and in caves.

OVERLEAF: Spectacular spiky soft corals add a splash of extra colour to many of the dive sites in the Swain Reefs.

For spectacular corals make sure you dive the pinnacle off the southern end of **Snake Reef**. This enormous coral structure rises from 35m and is decorated with beautiful gorgonians, sea whips, black coral trees and lovely sponges. Numerous caves and ledges cut into this pinnacle and provide a home to batfish, coral cod, angelfish, squirrelfish and dense schools of cardinalfish. This pinnacle is often visited by pelagic fish, but always in residence are the schools of fusiliers and surgeonfish.

A wonderful wall dive is found on the western side of **Heralds No.1**. This magic drop-off falls to depths beyond 30m and is encrusted with wonderful corals that are extremely photogenic. Take your time to explore the corals and many ledges as numerous small species are common, including nudibranchs, commensal shrimps, hawkfish, filefish, blennies, anemonefish, crayfish and thorny oysters. This drop-off is usually washed by currents so attracts a good range of reef and pelagic fish; expect to see turtles, Maori wrasse, coral trout, surgeonfish, parrotfish and batfish.

Central Reef has a lovely coral wall off its northern end that is alive with fish. Batfish, mackerel, sweetlips, coral trout and schools of snapper are a common sight. This wall drops to 30m and has many gorgeous soft corals, gorgonians and thick forests of sea whips. In the shallows at Central Reef divers will also find coral gardens and gutters to explore where turtles and small reef sharks like to hang out.

One of the best dive sites in the Swain Reefs is a towering bommie off the southern side of **Gannet Cay**. This immense bommie starts in 3m of water and drops into 35m. Large gorgonians, black coral trees, sea whips and soft corals decorate its walls, and these provide a home for hawkfish, damsels, coral cod and trumpetfish. This large pinnacle is always buzzing with fish life, including mackerel, trevally, barracuda, whitetip reef sharks and grey reef sharks.

Horseshoe Reef is one of the largest reef systems in the area and is surrounded by great dive sites. Wall dives are its main feature, with a continuous wall on its southern side dropping into 30m. Drifting along this wall is a real joy as the corals and fish life are both incredible and every now and then a large bommie looms out of the depths and begs to be explored. Giant Maori wrasse, trevally, sea snakes, reef sharks, sweetlips, coral trout, gropers and moray eels are just some of the species divers will encounter.

OPPOSITE, CLOCKWISE FROM TOP LEFT: Throughout the Swain Reefs divers will find lovely yellow featherstars clinging to the corals; many reef fish are curious of divers and will follow them around, including the lovely Diana's pigfish; numerous angelfish species are found on the Great Barrier Reef, but one of the prettiest is Meredith's angelfish; divers will encounter batfish at all the dive sites found in the Swain Reefs area.

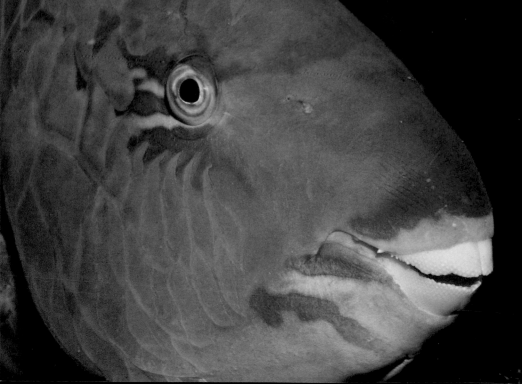

On the northern side of Horseshoe Reef is an extensive lagoon that is a very safe anchorage and a wonderful night dive. Only 10m deep, many small coral outcrops rise from the sandy sea floor and each one is packed with sleeping reef fish. But out on the prowl are crabs, shrimps, squid, sea snakes and many other critters.

Wall diving can be enjoy all around **Sanctuary Reef**. Typical of the area there are beautiful corals and healthy populations of reef fish, but the walls at Sanctuary Reef are a good spot to see a variety of nudibranchs and an abundance of anemones. Around three species of anemonefish are on show, but a closer look at these anemones will also reveal tiny commensal shrimps and porcelain crabs.

Hook Reef is a great spot for a relaxing dive through some magic coral gardens. Going no deeper than 15m divers can spend a lot of time admiring the hard corals or exploring the many nooks and crannies of the reef. Gropers, stingrays, barramundi cod, scorpionfish and olive sea snakes are just a few of the Hook Reef regulars.

The best feature of **Sinker Reef** is its incredible hard coral gardens in depths between 6m and 15m. The corals at this site are just exquisite, with a wide variety of plate corals, staghorn corals and brain corals. With plenty of bottom time spend a while to closely look at the corals to see Christmas tree tube worms, coral crabs, gobies, blennies, commensal shrimps and blue tangs. But also keep an eye out for the larger reef residents like barracuda, batfish and whitetip reef sharks.

Sandshoe Reef is typical of the Swain Reefs with wonderful coral gardens, sloping reef walls and many small bommies to explore. In depths to 25m divers will see coral trout, sweetlips, reef sharks, turtles and stingrays.

At the southern end of the Swain Reefs is **Hixson Cay**, which has a sheltered lagoon for night dives and a spectacular wall off its southern tip. This wall drops beyond 60m and is covered in lovely soft corals and gorgonians. With currents common, the pelagic action is full on, with trevally, mackerel, barracuda, rainbow runners and grey reef sharks charging along the wall. This wall is also home to coral trout, sweetlips, clown triggerfish and numerous gropers.

It is a pity that more charter boats don't visit the Swain Reefs, as this area certainly has some of the most interesting and varied diving on the entire Great Barrier Reef.

OPPOSITE TOP: Missed by many divers, the small Schultz's pipefish is often seen sitting on coral heads in the Swain Reefs.

OPPOSITE BOTTOM: Parrotfish have beak-like teeth as they feed by scrapping algae off rocks and hard coral.

SWAIN REEFS DIVE DATA

HOW TO GET THERE – A liveaboard charter boat is the only way to explore the Swain Reefs. Unfortunately very few trips are organised to this remote area. Charter boats that do explore this area generally depart from Bundaberg or Gladstone, both of which have regional airports.

BEST TIME TO VISIT – Year round

VISIBILITY – 12m to 30m.

CURRENTS – Strong and quite common.

WATER TEMPERTURE – Summer highs of 27°C to winter lows of 20°C.

ABOVE: Butterflyfish, like this redfin butterflyfish, truly are the butterflies of the reef, as they come in an amazing variety of colour patterns.

OPPOSITE: Divers will find the walls and bommies in the Swain Reefs adorned with many wonderful coral species.

— FEATURE —
POMPEY BLUE HOLES

Blue holes are mysterious deep circular reef depressions that are found in only a few locations around the world. The blue holes of the Bahamas and Belize are well known and very popular with divers, but few people realise that a number of blue holes are also found on the Great Barrier Reef in a remote area known as the Pompey Reef Complex.

The Pompey Reef Complex joins the northern end of the Swain Reefs and is a maze of reefs that is rarely visited. At least four blue holes are found in this area, which vary in size and depth. The blue holes on Cockatoo Reef and Molar Reef are the largest, and reported to be 240m to 295m in diameter and 30m to 40m deep. Another blue hole on Reef 20-374 is unsurveyed, but the blue hole on Neville Coleman Reef (formerly known as Reef 20-389) has been visited by charter boats and is the most spectacular.

This blue hole is around 100m in diameter and has sheer walls that drop to the bottom of the depression at 80m. The rim of the blue hole is a lovely coral garden, varying in depth from 1m to 15m, but the steep walls inside the blue hole are only sparsely decorated with corals, due to the water being quite still. A surprising number of fish reside in the blue hole, including Maori wrasse, batfish, trevally, coral trout and whitetip reef sharks.

Scientists have studied the blue holes at Cockatoo Reef and Molar Reef, and concluded that they were formed by karst erosion, a dissolution of the limestone structure that probably occurred over several low sea level events during the end of the last ice age. If closer to the mainland these blue holes would be a major tourist attraction, but located 200km offshore, they rarely see a visitor.

 Marion Reef

 Frederick Reef

Kenn Reef

Swain Reefs

 Saumarez Reef

 Wreck Reef

Rockhampton ⬤

| 0 | | 100 km |
| 0 | | 50 n mile |

SOUTHERN CORAL SEA REEFS

The reefs of the Southern Coral Sea offer the diver some of the most incredible adventure diving on the planet. These remote reefs are very different from the Northern Coral Sea Reefs, with the corals not growing to the gigantic sizes as they do in the north and with fewer dramatic wall dives. But the biggest difference is in the marine life, or one group of animals in particular – sea snakes, as the Southern Coral Sea Reefs are home to one of the largest populations of sea snakes found in the world.

Located well beyond the Great Barrier Reef, around 250km to 400km offshore, the Southern Coral Sea Reefs are one of the least visited regions in Australian waters. Naturally the only way to explore this area is on a liveaboard vessel, but very few charter boats venture to this remote region. This is very unfortunate for divers, as this area has some incredible diving with abundant marine life, beautiful healthy corals and the chance to explore virgin dive sites.

Sharks, rays, turtles, pelagic fish, gropers and a good variety of reef fish and invertebrate species await the diver prepared to venture to the Southern Coral Sea Reefs. But as already mentioned, the thing that makes this area special is sea snakes. On every dive on the reefs in this area divers will not just see one or two sea snakes, but dozens and sometimes hundreds of these marine reptiles. Four species of sea snake are common on these reefs, and every time a diver enters the water in this area you can expect to have these serpents following you around. This maybe a little unnerving at first, but divers quickly discover that the snakes are docile and pose no threat unless harassed, so learn to ignore the snakes or enjoy their company. The reefs of the Southern Coral Sea are a very unique part of Australia that are well worth diving if you can find a boat heading to this remote area.

Located 400km east of the Whitsunday coast, Marion Reef is the most

OPPOSITE: Schools of pyramid butterflyfish add a splash of colour to the dive sites at Marion Reef.

northerly and the most remote of the Southern Coral Sea Reefs. This spectacular reef is 40km long by 20km wide and has a deep lagoon at its centre full of colourful coral bommies. These bommies make for some spectacular diving, but divers will also find many coral gardens, channels, gutters and caves while exploring the main fringing reef at Marion Reef.

At **Northern Channels** divers can explore a maze of canyons, caves and bommies in depths between 15m and 30m. Beautiful hard corals and soft corals decorate this reef and divers will find whitetip reef sharks, grey reef sharks, turtles, moray eels, barracuda, parrotfish, coral trout and thick schools of snapper and pyramid butterflyfish. Of course sea snakes are found in large numbers, as they are at all the sites across Marion Reef.

Not far from the Northern Channels is a 10m tall pinnacle known as **Barra Bommie**. This wonderful bommie is found in 30m of water and is named for the school of hundreds of chevron barracuda that constantly circle above it. But these are not the only schooling fish here as thousands of stripey snapper and fusiliers also engulf this bommie and the surrounding reefs. Barra Bommie is a very photogenic coral outcrop as it is covered in gorgonians, sea whips and soft corals, and if divers search between the corals they will find moray eels, nudibranchs, sea stars, lionfish, scorpionfish and quite a few sea snakes. Swimming around this bommie are also reef sharks, dogtooth tuna, giant trevally and black-blotched stingrays.

Groper Channel is a spectacular drift dive on the central part of Marion Reef. This 25m deep channel cuts through the reef, joining the lagoon to the open ocean, and swarms with fish life. Divers drift by or swim with schools of trevally, drummer, fusiliers and sweetlips, plus numerous red bass, dogtooth tuna, barracuda, Maori wrasse, reef sharks and jobfish. Large gropers are often seen here, but are shy of divers, since they have rarely seen bubble blowing aliens. Groper Channel is dotted with small bommies, ridges and caves, and the strong currents have promoted the growth of luxuriate soft corals and gorgonians. There are probably plenty of invertebrate species to be seen in this channel, but with divers zooming along at one to two knots these smaller species are usually missed.

There are literally thousands of bommies in the lagoon at Marion Reef that rise from depths between 10m and 40m. Most of these bommies have never been dived, and only a handful have been given names. **Big Eye Bommie** is a tower of coral that rises from 25m to 5m and is riddled with ledges and

OPPOSITE TOP: Little blue damsels add a splash of colour to the greys and browns of most hard corals.

OPPOSITE BOTTOM: The turtle headed sea snake is an abundant species in the Southern Coral Sea, and feeding on fish eggs it is non-venomous.

OVERLEAF: A highlight of any dive in the Coral Sea is being surrounded by a school of chevron barracuda.

caves. This spectacular bommie is covered in pretty corals and home to dozens of sea snakes and a great variety of reef fish. The bommie's main attraction is a large school of bigeye trevally that constantly circle the structure, but schools of fusiliers and snapper are also common. This bommie is also a good place for divers to see grey reef sharks, coral trout, mackerel, dogtooth tuna, parrotfish, moray eels and coral cod.

Goat Mountain is another colourful lagoon bommie that rises from 30m to just below the surface. While Maori wrasse, moray eels, sweetlips, sea snakes, coral trout, rabbitfish and fusiliers are all common on this pinnacle, a major feature of the site is an extensive garden of pretty cabbage coral that swarms with thousands of yellow-fin goatfish. This spot is also a wonderful night dive with many shrimps and crabs emerging, and also numerous molluscs.

Frederick Reef is a small Coral Sea Reef that has been rarely visited by charter boats. This narrow reef is 10km long and has a prominent coral cay at its northern end that is dominated by a rocket-shaped lighthouse. Hundreds of sea birds nest on this tree-less cay, but the coral gardens off **North Cay** make for one of the best dive sites on this reef. Off North Cay divers can explore ridges of coral and many sand patches in depths to 20m. The sandy areas of this site are a good place to find stingrays and large white-spotted shovelnose rays. The pretty hard corals at North Cay are home to numerous reef fish and invertebrates, common species include anemonefish, surgeonfish, angelfish, butterflyfish, hawkfish and parrotfish. But many larger species gather here as well, with divers likely to encounter sea snakes, trevally, coral trout, barramundi cod, Maori wrasse, whitetip reef sharks, turtles and graceful spotted eagle rays.

Frederick Reef also has a large sandy lagoon with bommies scattered throughout in depths from 10m to 30m. None of these **Lagoon Bommies** have been named, and few of them have actually been dived, but they all provide for exciting diving. The best bommies are the ones found in deeper water, as they generally have the best coral growth and marine life. Soft corals, sea whips and gorgonians encrust the walls of these bommies and the corals provide a home to a diverse range of reef fish and invertebrates. Sea snakes are found in prolific numbers on these bommies, and with a very limited home range it is possible that they spend their entire life on a single bommie. Schools of snapper, goatfish, fusiliers and trevally gather on these bommies, but also common are reef sharks, turtles, stingrays and barracuda.

Saumarez Reef is a long reef, over 30km in length, and easy to see from a distance as a large shipwreck sits high and dry on this wonderful reef. This wreck

OPPOSITE TOP: A diver encounters a giant moray eel while diving Marion Reef.

OPPOSITE BOTTOM: Schools of yellow-fin goatfish swarm at the dive site known as Goat Mountain.

is the *Francis Preston Blair*, an American liberty ship that ran aground on the reef in 1945. It is a real pity this ship isn't underwater as it would make a spectacular wreck dive, but Saumarez Reef already has some spectacular dive sites.

At the northern end of the reef is **Northeast Cay**, one of the most amazing dive sites in the Southern Coral Sea. Off the western side of the cay are coral gardens and many coral ridges in depths to 20m. Many caves cut through these ridges, including a large swim-through cave. This cave is very colourful, with walls and ceiling lined with sponges and tubastra corals. The cave is also home to squirrelfish, bannerfish and sweetlips, and its many recesses are occupied by shrimps and crayfish. But this lovely cave is also a popular resting spot for black-blotched stingrays, tasselled wobbegong sharks and tawny nurse sharks.

The rest of the reef at Northeast Cay is packed with marine life with whitetip reef sharks, coral trout, turtles, Maori wrasse, batfish, moray eels, trevally, gropers, barracuda, jobfish and sea snakes all common. Eagle rays are often spotted cruising around the reef, but divers should also keep an eye on the ridge tops as tiger sharks also patrol this reef. Northeast Cay is an action packed dive site that you will want to do again and again.

Like many of the reefs of the Southern Coral Sea Saumarez Reef has a large lagoon where divers can explore countless **Coral Bommies**. With this lagoon reaching depths of 30m these bommies vary in size from only a few metres tall to giant 25m high towers of coral. The bigger the better generally, with the larger bommies attracting pelagic fish like trevally, mackerel, jobfish, dogtooth tuna, rainbow runners and barracuda. But most of these bommies are also populated with reef fish, gropers, reef sharks, turtles, stingrays and the ever present sea snakes.

Kenn Reef and **Cato Reef** are two small outposts that are rarely visited by dive charter boats. With most of these reefs hidden below the surface they are a shipping hazard and have claim a number of victims over the years. As little diving has been done on these reefs they have no established dive sites, and await the diver prepared to explore this little visited territory.

Wreck Reef is surrounded by spectacular dive sites, but like many reefs of the Southern Coral Sea it rarely gets a visitor. This 30km long reef has ensnared many ships over the years, included the *Cato* and *Porpoise* in 1803, while the ships were on a voyage to England with Australia's most famous explorer on board, Matthew Flinders. Around a dozen wrecks are scattered across Wreck Reef, but as most were timber ships they are broken up with little to see today. But divers come to Wreck Reef to explore pretty coral gardens and dramatic walls.

Porpoise Cay has a lovely coral garden off its northern side with gutters, ledges and caves to explore in depths to 15m. Crayfish, gropers, stingrays, squirrelfish, soldierfish and sweetlips can be found sheltering in the many caves in the area. But this reef is also a great place to encounter sea snakes, reef sharks, turtles, moray eels and prolific reef fish.

Caves are also a feature off **Bird Island**. Found in depths to 18m, some of these caves are 50m long and should only be explored by experienced divers. Residing in the many caves of Bird Island are stingrays, crayfish and large tawny nurse sharks. The coral gardens at Bird Island are also fascinating to explore as turtles, reef sharks, batfish, barracuda, sea snakes and anemonefish are all common.

The southern side of Wreck Reef offers the diver the best wall diving in the Southern Coral Sea. **Deep Finger** is the most dramatic site here, with the wall plummeting into 200m of water. Decorating this wall are pretty gorgonians, sea whips, soft corals and black coral trees. But with pelagic fish and sharks constantly patrolling this wall, the action is all in the blue water. Barracuda, trevally, dogtooth tuna, Spanish mackerel, bonito, batfish and rainbow runners cruise this wall, and between all these fish swim whitetip reef sharks and grey reef sharks. However, divers have also encountered tiger sharks and eagle rays at Deep Finger.

The reefs of the Southern Coral Sea maybe spectacular but they are largely unexplored and untouched. And it looks like it will remain this way unless more charter boats start offering trips to this amazing but remote region.

SOUTHERN CORAL SEA REEFS DIVE DATA

HOW TO GET THERE – A liveaboard boat is the only way to explore the Southern Coral Sea Reefs, but unfortunately very few boats venture to this region. Charter boats that do visit this area generally depart from Bundaberg or Gladstone, and both these cities have small regional airports.

BEST TIME TO VISIT – Year round, but being such a long way offshore this area is best avoided during the summer cyclone season.

VISIBILITY – 30m to 50m visibility is typical.

CURRENTS – Generally mild currents on most reefs, and none in the lagoons. But strong currents can be experienced in channels between the lagoon and open ocean.

WATER TEMPERTURE – Summer highs of 27°C to winter lows of 21°C.

— FEATURE —
SNAKES ALIVE

Some divers love them, other divers hate them, but it doesn't matter how you feel about sea snakes as there is little chance of avoiding them on many parts of the Great Barrier Reef. There are around 70 species of sea snake found in the seas of the Indo-Pacific region and about 14 species found on the Great Barrier Reef. The most common sea snake found throughout the region is the olive sea snake (*Aipysurus laevis*).

Olive sea snakes maybe one of the most venomous snakes in the world, but they also happen to be one of the most docile and placid, so pose little threat to divers. Olive sea snakes reach 2m in length and feed on fish and eels, and they seem to spend a great deal of their time looking for prey, searching in every nook and cranny.

Olive sea snakes are common throughout the entire Great Barrier Reef, but divers exploring the Southern Coral Sea Reefs will also come in contact with a few other species of these marine reptiles. The Dubois's sea snake (*Aipysurus duboisii*) has distinctive pale eyes and may only feed at night, as they are generally found sleeping during the day. The horned sea snake (*Acalyptophis peronii*) is an ambush predator that feed on gobies. This species is often observed lying on the bottom with its head near the entrance of goby holes. The cutest member of the sea snake family is the turtle headed sea snake (*Emydocephalus annulatus*), which do look a lot like a turtle. This is a non-venomous member of the family that feeds exclusively on fish eggs.

Almost all sea snakes are inquisitive and will come close to divers to 'check-them-out'. This can be unnerving for the first time, but divers just have to stay still and once the sea snake has satisfied its curiosity it will move on. Sea snakes pose no threat to divers unless handled or harassed, but are unique diving companions, especially on the reefs of the Southern Coral Sea.

OPPOSITE TOP: Olive sea snakes are common on the Great Barrier Reef.

OPPOSITE BOTTOM: The turtle headed sea snake is only seen in the Southern Coral Sea area.

Pleasant Island

North Keppel Island

Pumpkin Island
Sloping Island

Considine Bay

Man and Wife Rocks

Yeppoon

The Wall

Big Peninsula

Miall Island

Olive Point

The Child

Bald Rock

Barren Island

Middle Island

Great
Keppel
Island

The G

Underwater Observatory

Parkers Bommie

Halfway Island

Hannah Rock

Egg Rock

Humpy Island

Cathedral Rock

Pelican Island

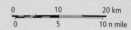

0   10   20 km
0   5   10 n mile

KEPPEL ISLANDS

The Keppel Islands offer the diver some of the most interesting and varied diving on the Great Barrier Reef. The 18 islands of the Keppel Group are located 15km off the coastal town of Yeppoon and are surrounded by coral reefs and surprisingly clear water.

The largest island of the Keppel Group is Great Keppel Island, which covers an area of 240 hectares and has over a dozen beautiful sandy beaches. Covered in thick forest and home to sea birds and many native animals, Great Keppel Island is the only island in the Keppel Group where visitors can stay, as the rest of the islands are protected as national park. The main resort on Great Keppel Island closed many years ago and several attempts to redevelop the resort have so far failed to get off the ground. However, visitors can stay on this picturesque island in more low key accommodation, such as tents, cabins and beach houses. The other option is to stay at one of the resorts or hotels on the mainland and visit the islands on day trips.

The rocky islands of the Keppel Group are surprisingly rich with corals and marine life, with turtles, schooling fish, sea snakes, sharks, rays and a good variety of nudibranchs seen in the area. Unfortunately commercial dive charters to the Keppel Group are no longer available, so the only way to dive this area is on a private boat. But if you do manage to organise a private boat there are over 40 wonderful dive sites awaiting to be explored at the lovely Keppel Islands.

Man and Wife Rocks is one of the most popular dive sites in the Keppel Group. Located north of Great Keppel Island, this rocky reef is covered in wonderful hard and soft corals and features a drop-off to 18m. Typical of the area this dive site is home to a great variety of reef fish – parrotfish, angelfish, wrasses, butterflyfish, hawkfish, surgeonfish, Moorish idols, triggerfish and many

OPPOSITE: Triplefin's are small reef fish that like to spend their time sitting in the coral.

more. But divers are also likely to encounter wobbegong sharks, moray eels, stingrays and olive sea snakes.

The most spectacular dive site at the Keppel Group would have to be at **Child Island**. This site can only be dived in calm conditions and divers will find coral gardens in the shallows with an abundance of marine life. The best dive site here is called **The Gulch**, which is a 30m deep channel between Child Island and Barren Island. The rocky walls of this channel are encrusted with lovely sea whips, gorgonians and soft corals, and with currents sweeping through The Gulch this site attracts pelagic visitors like trevally, barracuda, mackerel, batfish and cobia. Exploring this site divers are also likely to encounter wobbegong sharks, stingrays, eagle rays, sea snakes, giant Queensland gropers and maybe a manta ray.

Barren Island lives up to its name above water, but beneath the surface it is a different matter. This wonderful dive site is surrounded by pretty coral gardens that are dominated by hard corals. In depths to 15m divers will find a large variety of reef fish and also nudibranchs, moray eels, sea stars, shrimps, sea snakes and quite a few anemones with resident anemonefish and porcelain crabs.

Egg Rock is the most remote dive site at the Keppel Islands, but is well worth a look if you can get out to this isolated outcrop. With walls dropping to 30m that are covered in glorious corals, this is a very dramatic dive site. Schools of batfish, trevally and barracuda are often seen at Egg Rock, but this site is also home to coral trout, tawny nurse sharks, gropers, barramundi cod, turtles, sea snakes, sweetlips and wobbegong sharks.

Located at the northern end of Great Keppel Island is an excellent dive site called **Big Peninsula**. The rocky reef at this site is home to numerous reef fish and invertebrate species, but is also visited by pelagic fish and turtles. The reef can be explored in depths to 15m, and beyond this is a sandy bottom that is worth checking out. Sea whips sprout from the sand, and an interesting range of critters can be found here if you are prepared to have a look, such as flounders, shrimp gobies, octopus, snake eels, sea cucumbers, sea stars and flatheads.

Bald Rock is located off the eastern side of Great Keppel Island and is surrounded by rocky reefs in depths to 15m. The corals at this site are very photogenic, with gorgonians, soft corals, ascidians and sponges colouring the reef. This is a good spot to search for nudibranchs as over a dozen species can be found on a good day, including the large and impressive Spanish dancer. Also common at Bald Rock are sweetlips, lionfish, scorpionfish, batfish and moray eels.

OPPOSITE TOP: The orbicular porcupinefish can blow up like a balloon if threatened or harassed.

OPPOSITE BOTTOM: The common coral trout is a popular target for fishers, so are generally only seen in protected green zones.

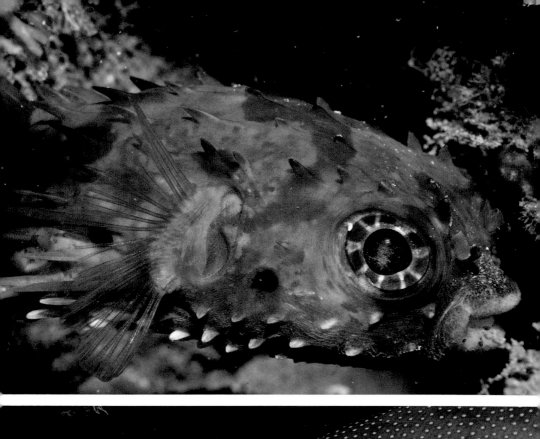

Off the northern side of Miall Island is a lovely dive site called **The Wall**. The sloping wall at this site varies in depth from 5m to 14m and is covered in soft corals, anemones, sponges and ascidians. While reef fish and a few larger species can be seen, this is a good spot for macro photography as flatworms, shrimps, hermit crabs, juvenile fish and nudibranchs are common.

Middle Island is located on the inner, western side of Great Keppel Island, so is a very sheltered spot that is popular with snorkelers and divers. **Olive Point** is a wonderful site with fringing coral reef in depths to 14m. Staghorn corals dominate the reef, and divers will find blue spotted lagoon rays, angelfish, lionfish, batfish and moray eels.

The **Underwater Observatory** at Middle Island makes for an interesting dive in only 6m of water as a great variety of fish linger under this structure. Schools of sweetlips, snappers, damsels, sergeant majors, wrasses, rabbitfish and trevally all gather at this site. A number of gropers also hang out here, but keep an eye out for moray eels, stingrays and sea snakes.

One of the best dive sites in the Keppel Group is **Parkers Bommie**, located off the south-eastern tip of Great Keppel Island. This wonderful bommie rises from 17m to just below the surface and is surrounded by a beautiful rocky reef. Gorgonians, sea whips, sponges and soft corals decorate this reef, providing food and shelter for a great range of reef fish and nudibranchs. Olive sea snakes are a common companion at this site, but divers will also encounter wobbegong sharks, stingrays, trevally, batfish, sweetlips, gropers and even the odd manta ray.

South of Great Keppel Island is a rocky lump known as Humpy Island, which is the location of a brilliant dive site called **Cathedral Rock**. This site has a wonderful terrain of gutters, ledges and caves that any diver will enjoy exploring. Covered in corals, this site doesn't get many big visitors, but divers will find crayfish, crabs, egg cowries and nudibranchs.

There are dozens of other dive sites found at the Keppel Islands, and with only small numbers of divers venturing to this area on their own private boats, you can almost guarantee you will never have a crowd.

OPPOSITE TOP: The honeycomb moray eel is often seen at the Keppel Group.

OPPOSITE BOTTOM: Spindle cowries are not seen by many divers, but they can be found clinging to gorgonian fans in the Keppel Group.

KEPPEL ISLANDS DIVE DATA

HOW TO GET THERE – Rockhampton is the closest city to the Keppel Islands that has an airport, and is located 40km west of Yeppoon. A ferry service to Great Keppel Island departs daily from Rosslyn Bay, just south of Yeppoon. Unfortunately at the time of publication no dive charters are operating in this area.

BEST TIME TO VISIT – Year round.

VISIBILITY – 10m to 15m on average, but can be over 20m on the outer islands.

CURRENTS – Can be strong around some of the islands, but most diving is done in sheltered locations.

WATER TEMPERTURE – Summer highs of 27°C to winter lows of 20°C.

ABOVE: Wonderful multi-coloured nudibranchs are very common at the Keppel Group.

OPPOSITE: Brown spotted gropers are a shy species and will often hide in caves or amongst the corals.

– FEATURE –

CLEANING STATIONS

Fish take grooming very seriously. As a fashionable fish you can't be seen with loose scales, flaky skin or an isopod hanging from your fin. And god-forbid you being caught with food stuck between your teeth. To solve these grooming issues fish visit their local beautician, also known as a cleaning station.

Cleaning stations are common on almost every patch of reef on the Great Barrier Reef. The most obvious ones are those operated by common cleaner wrasse (*Labroides dimidiatus*). Teams of these tiny wrasse, growing to only 12cm in length, establish cleaning stations on bommies and other coral outcrops.

Reef fish queue up at cleaning stations and let the cleaners know that they are ready for a service by opening their mouth, or hovering in place. Then the cleaners go into action, usually two or three cleaners per fish, they even enter the mouth and gills of their customers. It usually only takes a few minutes to clean each fish, but when a larger client arrives, like a manta ray, groper or reef shark, all the other customers get put on hold and several teams go to work.

Common cleaner wrasse are so popular that no one eats them, which the sabre-tooth blenny (*Aspidontus taeniatus*) has used to its advantage. This sneaky fish mimics the cleaner wrasse, by looking and behaving the same, which allows it to get close to unsuspecting fish and take a nip of flesh out of them.

Around 50 other fish species are known to provide cleaning duties at some stage of their life cycle. Surgeonfish, which like to eat algae, also set up turtle cleaning stations so they can remove the algae off the shells of turtles.

Revival cleaning stations are run by shrimps. These are generally harder to find as they prefer the shelter of a cave or ledge, and they don't seem to get as many customers as the cleaner wrasse. White-banded cleaner shrimps (*Lysmata amboinensis*) are the most common cleaner shrimps, but many shrimp species provide this service.

Moray eels in particular use the services of cleaner shrimps and often share a hole in the reef, which gives them the exclusive use of the shrimps as other fish are not game to get close to a moray. These shrimps enjoy cleaning so much that they will also clean a diver if you place your hand in front of them. Some divers even remove their regulator to allow the shrimps to floss their teeth.

Cleaning stations are a very important part of the Great Barrier Reef and are always entertaining to watch.

OPPOSITE TOP: A cleaner shrimp delicately cleans the jaw of a giant moray eel.

OPPOSITE BOTTOM: A small cleaner wrasse services a diagonal-banded sweetlips.

North Reef Island

Tryon Island

Broomfield Reef

Heron Island
Sykes Reef
Wistari Reef

Masthead Island
Polmaise Reef

Lamont Reef

Fitzroy Reef

Llewellyn Reef

Boult Reef

Hoskyn Islands

Fairfax Islands

Lady Musgrave Island

Bustard Bay

Lady Elliot Island

Snake Pit

0   10   20 km
0   5   10 n mile

CAPRICORN & BUNKER GROUPS

The magnificent reefs and coral cays of the Capricorn and Bunker Groups are a very special part of the Great Barrier Reef. Located at the southern end of the Great Barrier Reef, right on the Tropic of Capricorn, the 16 coral cays in this area are an important nesting site for turtles and sea birds, while the 22 reefs of the group offer exceptional diving.

The Capricorn and Bunker Group are the best location on the Great Barrier Reef to see 'big stuff' – as these reefs are home to manta rays, turtles, leopard sharks, reef sharks, shovelnose rays, gropers, eagle rays, stingrays, wobbegong sharks and tawny nurse sharks. All these animals are seen elsewhere on the Great Barrier Reef, but for some reason there appears to be a higher density of them in this area, especially manta rays and turtles. Of course there is also plenty of smaller stuff to be seen, making for some great diving.

You have many options when it comes to exploring the Capricorn and Bunker Groups. Two of the islands have well established resorts, Heron Island and Lady Elliot Island, and are world famous for their diving. Divers can also visit Lady Musgrave Island on a day trip, and camping is even available on several of the islands. But the best way to explore this area is on a liveaboard charter boat. Twenty years ago a dozen charter boats were exploring this area, but these days only a few liveaboards visit this region. Anyway you choose to dive the Capricorn and Bunker Groups expect to experience some incredible diving.

North Reef, as its name suggests, is at the northern end of the Capricorn Group. Manta rays are often observed cruising around this reef, but you can never guarantee an encounter. One of the best dive sites at North Reef is off its northern side where divers can explore a coral wall and numerous gutters in depths to 20m. This lovely reef is a great spot to see batfish, trevally, snappers and Maori wrasse. Investigating the many ledges here will reward the diver with sightings of

OPPOSITE: Radiant tubastra coral prefers to grow in caves, and opens at night to feed.

moray eels, crayfish, pufferfish and tasselled wobbegong sharks. Other marine life encountered at North Reef includes turtles, stingrays and reef sharks.

Tryon Island is surrounded by wonderful dive sites, but the best of these would have to be the bommie fields on the western side of the island. These large coral heads are found in depths from 10m to 20m and are home to a great diversity of life. A close inspection of any of these bommies will reveal pipefish, nudibranchs, lionfish, scorpionfish and many crustaceans, but these bommies also attract reef sharks, turtles, coral trout, sweetlips and manta rays.

Broomfield Reef is rarely dived even though it does have lovely coral gardens and numerous bommies on its northern and western sides. In depths to 18m divers will see sweetlips, snappers, coral trout, parrotfish, barracuda, cobia and the usual assortment of smaller reef fish.

East of Heron Island is a great place to dive called **Sykes Reef**. Exposed in rough conditions, so not often dived, Sykes Reef has a series of gutters off its northern and eastern sides that are often overflowing with baitfish. In depths from 12m to 18m divers will encounter batfish, eagle rays, turtles, moray eels, surgeonfish, trevally and gropers. Sykes Reef also has a good contingent of sharks; bottom dwelling tasselled wobbegongs and tawny nurse sharks rest under ledges, while patrolling the reef are whitetip reef sharks and grey reef sharks. If you can get out to Sykes Reef it is a spectacular dive.

Masthead Island is one of the most popular camping locations in the Capricorn Group, but as compressors are not allowed, the reefs surrounding this island are mostly enjoyed by snorkelers. Typical of the reefs in the area there are lovely coral gardens in the shallows off the northern and western sides of the island, and in deeper water numerous bommies. Common species seen here include turtles, reef sharks, stingrays, parrotfish, batfish and a multitude of smaller colourful reef fish.

Polmaise Reef is named after a ship of the same name that grounded on this reef in 1873. Not often dived, as it is quite an exposed reef, one of the best sites to explore on Polmaise Reef is a collection of small bommies at the northwest end of the reef. Only 12m deep and usually washed by currents, the corals at this site are quite lovely and support a good selection of reef fish and invertebrate species. Divers will see wobbegongs, turtles, sweetlips, gropers, snappers, coral trout and the odd sea snake at these bommies.

Lamont Reef is the most northern reef of the Bunker Group and has a

OPPOSITE TOP: A school of hussars gather at the base of a bommie. This species is very common around the Capricorn & Bunker Groups.

OPPOSITE BOTTOM: Big-fin reef squid are occasionally seen by day, but divers are more likely to see them night diving the Capricorn & Bunker Groups.

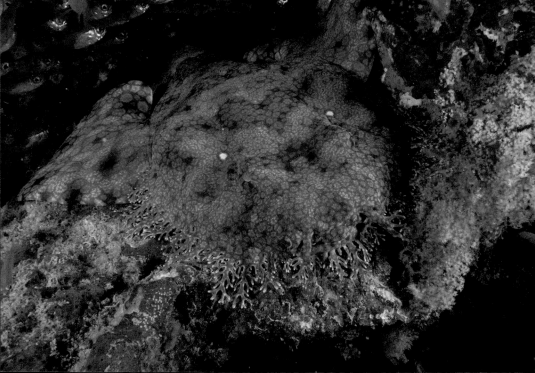

great drop-off on its southern side. This wall drops from 15m to 25m and is riddled with caves, ledges and gutters. Gorgonians, sea whips, sponges and black coral trees colour this wall and divers are likely to see nudibranchs, boxfish, moray eels and hawkfish. Olive sea snakes appear to be common at Lamont Reef, but divers will also see red emperors, coral trout, coral cod, whitetip reef sharks and giant trevally.

Fitzroy Reef is such a large reef that it has a lagoon at its centre that is a popular overnight anchorage and night diving location. Off its northern side are numerous bommies in depths to 18m that are always a pleasure to explore. Residents of these bommies include Maori wrasse, barramundi cod, moray eels and coral trout, but also keep an eye out for reef sharks, turtles and stingrays. Fitzroy Reef is generally a wonderful location for macro photography as nudibranchs, juvenile boxfish, octopus, lizardfish, hawkfish, gobies and blennies are all common.

The northwest side of **Llewellyn Reef** has many lovely dive sites, including a site called **The Catacombs**. A wall dropping from 15m to 30m is the main feature here, but as it is cut by numerous ledges and caves it is a wonderful spot to explore. Decorating this wall are black coral trees and gorgonians, while the caves are lined with pretty lace corals and tubastra corals. This is the kind of spot where you can either look for smaller critters on the wall or larger stuff out wide. Common are coral trout, lionfish, rock cods, nudibranchs, parrotfish and wrasses, while off the wall divers will see turtles, mackerel, barracuda, trevally, reef sharks and even mobula rays.

The most popular dive site at **Boult Reef** is the extensive coral gardens on the northwest side of this small reef. In depths to 15m divers can explore gutters and small coral heads where turtles, trevally, moray eels, rainbow runners and sweetlips are found. Manta rays often visit Boult Reef, so keep an eye on the surface as they swim overhead feeding on plankton.

Hoskyn Islands is another small reef of the Bunker Group, but it is a great place to encounter manta rays. Countless bommies dot the bottom on the northern side of this reef, which seem to attract passing manta rays. These bommies are found in depths from 12m to 20m, and each has its own community of fish. Drifting from bommie to bommie is a great way to see reef sharks, stingrays, turtles, trevally, coral trout, Maori wrasse and even the odd leopard shark.

OPPOSITE TOP: One of the cutest fish seen on the Great Barrier Reef is the juvenile yellow boxfish.

OPPOSITE BOTTOM: Tasselled wobbegong sharks are particular common on the reefs and bommies of the Capricorn and Bunker Groups.

The greatest collection of bommies in the Bunker Group is found off the northwest side of **Fairfax Islands**. Rising from depths between 12m and 20m, the largest of the bommies off Fairfax Islands will keep you occupied for an entire dive. Many of these bommies stand over 8m tall and are like a giant chunk of Swiss cheese, riddled with ledges and caves that are generally packed with cardinalfish or glassfish. Giant moray eels, tasselled wobbegongs, crayfish and gropers claim these bommies as homes, but divers are also likely to see reef sharks, turtles, stingrays, leopard sharks, eagle rays, pelagic fish and manta rays around these wonderful bommies.

There are a number of deeper shoals around the Capricorn and Bunker Groups that are rarely dived, but there is one that is definitely worth checking out called Herald Patches. Located south of Lady Elliot Island, Herald Patches is actually the southern most point of the Great Barrier Reef. This reef rises from 45m to 20m and is a mix of gutters, ridges and ledges. There are some pretty corals to be seen here, but the main feature is sea snakes, as this is the **Snake Pit**.

It is easy to see how this dive site got its name as the bottom literally seethes with sea snakes. Olive sea snakes and banded sea snakes are seen at this site in their hundreds; they can be seen swimming around the reef, sliding into holes or heading to the surface for air. But this site is also a magnet for fish life, with schools of snappers, sweetlips, batfish, barracuda, trevally and fusiliers swarming here. Divers will also see gropers, Maori wrasse, eagle rays and reef sharks at this spectacular dive site.

CAPRICORN AND BUNKER GROUP DIVE DATA

HOW TO GET THERE – The only way to explore the reefs of the Capricorn and Bunker Groups is from a liveaboard charter boat, these generally depart from Bundaberg or Gladstone, both these cities have smaller regional airports.

BEST TIME TO VISIT – Year round, the islands and reefs of the Capricorn and Bunker Groups provide very sheltered diving in most weather conditions.

VISIBILITY – 15m to 30m generally.

CURRENTS – Mild currents are common around the island and often used to do drift dives.

WATER TEMPERTURE – Summer highs of 27°C to winter lows of 19°C.

OPPOSITE: One of the largest shark species seen on the Great Barrier Reef is the tawny nurse shark. They are a very docile species and spend most of the day sleeping in caves.

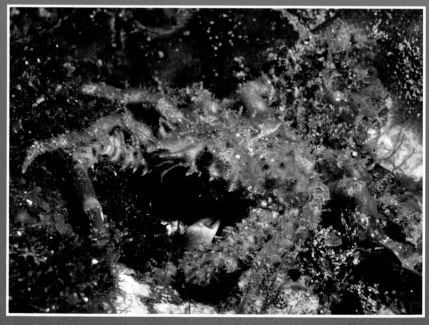

– FEATURE –
CREATURES OF THE NIGHT

Night diving on the Great Barrier Reef exposes the diver to a whole new world of creatures that are not generally seen during daylight hours. The islands and reefs of the Capricorn and Bunker Groups are a great location for night diving as you not only see the animals that shelter amongst the coral, but also the strange creatures that emerge from the sand after dark.

Numerous mollusc species appear at night to feed, such as cone shells, cowries and volutes, but after dark divers are also more likely to see squid and octopus. While most reef fish sleep at night, others are far more active as they stalk the reef for food; keep an eye out for moray eels, whitetip reef sharks, barracuda and trevally.

But the reef at night really belongs to the crustaceans, the crabs, shrimps and crayfish. These armour plated critters feed, fight and mate at night, and on some reefs you will see thousands of tiny eyes as you wave your torch around. Keep an eye out for hermit crabs, boxer shrimps, painted crayfish, spider crabs, hingebeak shrimps, marble shrimps and coral crabs as you explore this coral wonderland by night.

OPPOSITE TOP: After sunset an incredible range of shells emerge from the sand to feed.

OPPOSITE BOTTOM: Spider crabs are another species that appears upon night fall.

ABOVE: One of the more unusual hermit crab species seen at night attaches sea anemones to its home as a form of protection.

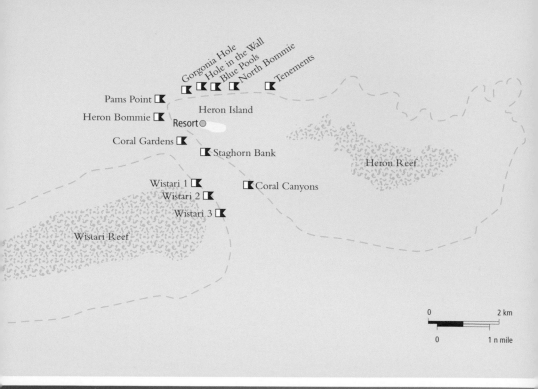

Gorgonia Hole
Hole in the Wall
Blue Pools
North Bommie
Tenements

Pams Point

Heron Island

Heron Bommie

Resort

Coral Gardens

Staghorn Bank

Heron Reef

Wistari 1

Wistari 2

Coral Canyons

Wistari 3

Wistari Reef

0   2 km

0   1 n mile

HERON ISLAND

Tourism on the Great Barrier Reef started in the 1880s, when a handful of boats started offering day trips to this coral wonderland. But the potential of the reef as a tourism attraction wasn't realised until a resort opened on Heron Island in the 1930s. The resort slowly grew in popularity, especially after the birth of scuba diving in the 1950s, when Heron Island became the most popular place to dive on the Great Barrier Reef. Today Heron Island is still a fabulous place to dive, as its surrounding waters are a haven for marine life.

Located in the heart of the Capricorn Group, Heron Island is situated 80km east of Gladstone. The island is covered in a jungle of pisonia trees, which provide a home for millions of nesting sea birds. There are so many birds on this lovely island that everyone that visits gets pooped on at least once during their holiday, almost like a welcoming gift from above.

While sitting on a large reef, Heron Island is actually a small coral cay, only 16 hectares in area, and a stroll around the island can be completed in 20 minutes. While the great majority of the island is heavily wooded and national park, the western end of the island accommodates a wonderful resort and a research station operated by the University of Queensland. The Heron Island Resort today is a lot more upmarket than when it opened in the 1930s, and today has a range of comfortable cabins, a pool, restaurant and other facilities. To get to the island guests have a choice of boat or seaplane, and on arrival guests are greeted by the iconic *HMCS Protector,* a wreck that forms a breakwater at the entrance to the harbour.

Heron Island is without question a divers' paradise, but the island also has some of the best snorkelling on the Great Barrier Reef – on its reef flats, on the reef edge and even in the harbour. This is one place where you don't go for a sleep or hit the bar after a dive. You drop your tank and go for a snorkel to look

OPPOSITE: A group of green turtles rest on the famous Heron Bommie, Heron Island.

for reef sharks, lemon sharks, shovelnose rays, schools of stingrays and gorgeous epaulette sharks, species that are generally not seen while on scuba. But snorkelers will also see abundant fish life, manta rays, eagle rays and even turtles.

Turtles are particularly common at Heron Island as the island is a nesting spot for several species of these marine reptiles. Turtles are in fact what attracted people to Heron Island in the first place, not to view them, but to kill and eat them, with a turtle processing plant established in the 1920s. Fortunately the processing plant wasn't a success and closed down after only a few years. Today turtles are fully protected and seen in abundance at every dive site around this magic island.

All of the popular dive sites at Heron Island are located around the western end of the extensive Heron Reef, but a few are also found on nearby Wistari Reef, which is only separated from Heron Island by a narrow channel. Over twenty dive sites are found around Heron Island, and good news for those that get seasick is that most of the sites are only five to ten minutes from the harbour.

Positioned just outside the harbour is one of Heron Island's most famous dive sites, the legendary **Heron Bommie**. This group of six large bommies is always a brilliant dive, with masses of fish and many other fascinating critters. Located on a sandy slope, the bommies are found in depths from 8m to 18m, and are always swarming with fish. Sweetlips, gropers, batfish, coral trout, barramundi cod, snappers, coral cod, hussars, emperors, trevally, parrotfish, surgeonfish, tuskfish and barracuda are just some of the species seen in vast numbers.

But Heron Bommie is also home to whitetip reef sharks, moray eels, stingrays, turtles, spotted eagle rays and tasselled wobbegong sharks. The bommies are actually a giant cleaning station and it is fascinating to watch the fish queueing up to get cleaned. But it is even better when a massive manta ray arrives to prevail itself of this service.

At first glance these giant bommies look devoid of colourful corals, but if divers investigate the many ledges and caves that cut through these coral heads they will find them decorated with soft corals, sponges and tubastra corals. There are also no shortage of invertebrate species, with shrimps, crabs, sea stars, flatworms and nudibranchs to be seen. Heron Bommie is a brilliant dive site where photographers will have a field day.

Pams Point is another excellent dive site where divers can explore pretty coral gardens or another great batch of bommies. Only 150m from Heron Bommie, Pams Point has much the same marine life, but not in the same

OPPOSITE TOP: A diver explores one of the colourful caves at Heron Bommie.

OPPOSITE BOTTOM: Green turtles are seen on every dive at Heron Island, as they nest on the island each summer.

numbers. In depths to 20m divers will encounter pelagic fish, turtles, stingrays, eagle rays and a manta ray or two if lucky.

Off the northern side of Heron Island is a wonderful coral canyon called **Gorgonia Hole**. This site varies in depth from 12m to 20m, and features many caves, ledges and crevasses for divers to explore. Gorgonia Hole is covered in many varieties of hard coral and soft coral, however a highlight of the site are the exquisite gorgonian fans. Reef fish, crayfish, nudibranchs, turtles, reef sharks, gropers and stingrays are all seen at this popular dive site.

Hole in the Wall is named for just that, a large hole in the coral wall. But divers exploring this wall will find plenty of other caves and ledges to investigate. This wall drops into 14m, and off the wall are numerous small bommies. Sweetlips, trevally, gropers, stingrays, turtles and moray eels are just some of the creatures encountered.

Blue Pools is a popular snorkelling spot, as this large cove in the reef is shallow and sheltered, but also buzzing with reef fish. But for divers the wall outside Blue Pools is of more interest. Dropping to 15m, this lovely wall is adorned with pretty corals and visited by pelagic fish, including trevally, barracuda and mackerel. Divers are also likely to see batfish, stingrays, eagle rays and reef sharks.

North Bommie is another collection of fabulous coral heads off the north side of Heron Island. The bommies at this site are found in depths from 12m to 20m and like all bommies off Heron Island are a haven for marine life. Schools of baitfish and glassfish swell the caves at this site and provide a feast for trevally, coral trout and barramundi cod. Also common at North Bommie are turtles, tasselled wobbegongs, lionfish, squirrelfish, tuskfish, surgeonfish and sweetlips. Manta rays often appear at this site, but don't forget to look for smaller critters, as pipefish, boxfish, filefish, shrimps and leaf scorpionfish await the diver with a keen eye.

Tenements is another area of canyons and bommies where divers will find a wonderful array of marine life. Going no deeper than 18m, divers will encounter reef sharks, turtles, schools of snapper and good numbers of pelagic fish.

The dive sites off the southern side of Heron Island experience more currents, washing through the narrow Wistari Channel. But these currents mean that the corals are very rich and the fish life prolific. The **Coral Gardens** is one of the most popular sites in this area, with a wall, ledges and naturally some lovely coral gardens to explore. Take a torch on this dive to explore the many

OPPOSITE TOP: A number of pretty gorgonian fans can be seen at Wistari 1.

OPPOSITE LEFT: Indian seastars feed on algae and are often seen around Heron Island.

OPPOSITE RIGHT: A diver encounters a large pinnate batfish at Heron Bommie.

ledges that undercut the wall, as turtles, crayfish, gropers, moray eels, tasselled wobbegongs and tawny nurse sharks are often found residing in the darkness. Drifting this coral wall divers are also likely to encounter reef sharks, trevally, snapper, barracuda, gropers and the odd manta ray.

The **Staghorn Bank** is a continuation of the Coral Gardens, with the reef here dominated by groves of staghorn coral. Green and hawksbill turtles are often seen at this site, alongside whitetip reef sharks, parrotfish and trevally. Not far from this site is the **Coral Canyons**, where divers can explore deep gutters and several bommies in depths to 20m. Turtles, reef sharks and all the regular reef fish are seen at this site, but schools of squid often make an appearance at the Coral Canyons.

There are many other wonderful dive sites around Heron Island that are just as good as the ones listed, such as **The Junction**, **Plate Ledge**, **Coral Grotto**, **Turtle Gully**, **Ned's Bommie**, **Libbies Lair** and **Coral Cascades**.

The nearby Wistari Reef also has some excellent dive sites, with wall diving a feature. The **Wistari Wall** (simply known as Wistari 1, Wistari 2 or Wistari 3 depending on where you dive) drops from 3m to 20m and is often done as a drift dive. The corals along the wall are good in some spots and average in others, but divers will find numerous reef fish, invertebrates and pelagic fish to keep them entertained. Coral trout, trevally, jobfish, fusiliers, sweetlips, Maori wrasse, hussars, emperors, gropers, mackerel, batfish and barracuda are just some of the common fish species. Whitetip reefs sharks are generally observed resting at the base of the wall, but divers will also encounter turtles, stingrays, manta rays and even olive sea snakes.

A spot that is not often dived, but is brilliant if you want to see masses of fish and rays, is a dive in the **Heron Harbour**. Only 3m to 5m deep, the best location is right under the jetty, as mingling here are hundreds of sweetlips, rabbitfish, trevally and several gropers. The sandy bottom under the jetty is usually covered in numerous stingrays and shovelnose rays, but also common are blacktip reef sharks and eagle rays. This is a great spot on either scuba or snorkel, but access times are restricted to early morning or late afternoon, to avoid boat traffic.

Heron Island is a very special part of the Great Barrier Reef and one visit is never enough, with many divers returning year after year to once again experience the magic of this wonderful destination.

OPPOSITE: Heron Harbour is a wonderful place to snorkel or dive, especially under the jetty as many species of rays gather here, including rare porcupine rays.

HERON ISLAND DIVE DATA

HOW TO GET THERE – Heron Island is located near the town of Gladstone, which is serviced by domestic flights. From Gladstone visitors travel to Heron Island by boat or seaplane.

BEST TIME TO VISIT – Year round the diving is excellent at Heron Island.

VISIBILITY – 12m to 25m.

CURRENTS – Mild to strong currents are common around the island and often used to do drift dives.

WATER TEMPERTURE – Summer highs of 27°C to winter lows of 19°C.

– FEATURE –
TIMELESS TURTLES

Turtles have been swimming the oceans of the world for over 150 million years. These ancient reptiles are common on the Great Barrier Reef, with six of the seven known species seen in this area, but only three of these species are usually encountered by divers.

The most common species in reef waters is the green turtle (*Chelonia mydas)* which reaches a length of 1.5m and can weigh up to 130kg. The green turtle is the only herbivorous turtle, with their diet made up of sea grasses and algae. While observed on almost any reef in this region, the largest numbers of green turtles are encountered around the islands where they breed and lay eggs. Raine Island is the largest green turtle rookery in the world, but large numbers of green turtles also nest on the islands of the Capricorn and Bunker Groups.

The loggerhead turtle (*Caretta caretta*) is a very distinctive turtle with its rather large head. This species, like all turtle species, is highly migratory and studies have shown they travel from country to country, some have even crossed the Pacific Ocean. The loggerhead turtle grows to 1m in length and feeds on crabs, urchins, sponges, anemones, molluscs and sea jellies, which often sees them consuming plastic bags by mistake. This species prefers cooler subtropical waters, so are far more common on southern reefs.

ABOVE: Loggerhead turtles are more commonly seen in southern reef waters.

OPPOSITE: The hawksbill turtle is the smallest species found on the Great Barrier Reef.

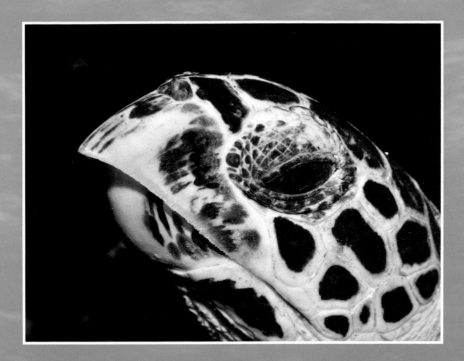

The hawksbill turtle (*Eretmochelys imbricata*) grows to 1m in length and enjoys a diet of sea jellies, anemones and especially sponges. This species is often confused with the green turtle, but hawksbill turtles have a more pronounced beak and its shell plates overlap. The world's largest population of hawksbill turtles reside on the Great Barrier Reef, but with a population of only a few thousand, encounters are still rare.

Turtles live for around 80 years and most species don't breed until they are at least 30 years of age. Female turtles nest every two to three years, returning to the same beach where they hatched. Females lay several egg clutches in a season, up to 100 eggs, then leave the eggs in the warm sand to hatch. The young turtles emerge 12 weeks later and have to fend for themselves. They enter the water and disappear into the open ocean and don't return to the Great Barrier Reef until they are over 20cm in length.

Turtle populations around the world are under threat, with all species listed as either endangered or vulnerable. Their populations have greatly declined over the last century due to hunting, pollution and habitat loss. The Great Barrier Reef is one of the most important turtle habitats in the world, but with these ancient reptiles undertaking long migrations to neighbouring countries they leave the safe waters of the reef into an unknown fate.

Entrance Bommie ◪

Musgrave Channel ◪

◪ Lady Musgrave Lagoon

Coral Gardens ◪
The Canyons ◪

Radar Fix ◪

Lady Musgrave Island

Manta Ray Bommie ◪

Lady Musgrave Reef

◪ The Drop Off

0   2 km

0   1 n mile

LADY MUSGRAVE ISLAND

ady Musgrave Island is a pretty coral cay located at the western end of a huge reef and lagoon, over 2900 hectares in size. This lovely island is covered in a thick forest of pisonia trees where thousands of sea birds roost. Its surrounding reef is home to turtles, sharks, pelagic fish and manta rays. Besides diving and snorkelling you can do one thing on Lady Musgrave Island that is unique, you can camp on the island. Lady Musgrave Island is one of the few islands where camping is permitted, allowing visitors to waking each morning to find the clear waters of the Great Barrier Reef only metres away.

Facilities on Lady Musgrave Island are very basic, just a toilet block, so if you do decide you want to camp on the Great Barrier Reef, ensure you can carry all your gear and food with you. Also book your camping permit well in advance, as numbers are limited and get snatched up very quickly. Most campers only bring snorkelling gear with them, but groups from Dive Clubs often stay on the island and bring their own compressor and boat, so they can explore the reef at their own pace. But there are far easier ways to dive Lady Musgrave Island.

Liveaboard boats occasionally visit Lady Musgrave Island, as there are many wonderful dive sites right around this island, plus the lagoon is a very safe overnight anchorage. However, the easiest way to dive Lady Musgrave Island is on a day trip from the town of Seventeen Seventy. Lady Musgrave Cruises visit the island daily, allowing campers on and off, and day trippers the chance to explore the island, snorkel the lagoon, or for divers to explore the many brilliant dive sites around this magic island.

One of the most iconic dive sites at Lady Musgrave Island is located at the western tip of the reef, a brilliant site called **Manta Ray Bommie**. This name is a bit misleading as there are actually dozens of bommies at this site, and usually quite a few manta rays as well. These giant rays can be seen almost

OPPOSITE: The calm waters inside Lady Musgrave Lagoon allow delicate corals to flourish.

anywhere around the island, but especially favour the bommies at this site as they are cleaning stations. The winter months are usually the best time to see large numbers of manta rays, up to a dozen at times, but even seeing one or two gliding slowly around a bommie while cleaner wrasse go to work is a memorable experience.

The bommies at this site are found in depths between 15m and 22m, and vary greatly in size. The largest bommies are decorated with gorgonians and riddled with ledges and caves, which can be full of baitfish. At Manta Ray Bommie divers will also encounter turtles, stingrays, whitetip reef sharks, moray eels, sweetlips, coral trout, barramundi cod, batfish and all the usual reef fish. At the end of your dive also have a look at the coral gardens in shallower water as many green turtles use this area to rest.

The reef on the northwest side of Lady Musgrave Island has a number of dive sites with names like **Radar Fix**, **The Canyons** and **Coral Gardens**. These sites are all very similar with extensive fields of hard coral in the shallows and as one dives deeper gutters and bommies can be explored. You generally don't have to go any deeper than 18m to have a great dive in this area as there is plenty to see and photograph. As much of this area is a green zone, where fishing is not allowed, you can expect to see abundant fish life. Maori wrasse are generally only seen in this area of the island, but divers will also encounter barramundi cod, batfish, coral trout, sweetlips, rabbitfish, emperors and snappers. Turtles, reef sharks, stingrays and schools of trevally are also common.

Adjacent to the channel that allows boats access to the Lady Musgrave Lagoon is a large blade of coral called **Entrance Bommie**. This bommie sits in 23m of water and is cut by numerous ledges and caves, which attract a wealth of marine life. Schools of sweetlips and snapper congregate here, but also common are gropers, coral trout and a good collection of angelfish. Tawny nurse sharks often rest in this area, but divers will also encounter reef sharks, eagle rays and stingrays.

One of the most exciting dives at Lady Musgrave Island is a drift dive on an incoming tide into the lagoon. **Musgrave Channel** is only 13m deep, but as you zoom along at one or two knots you will have a ball watching all the fish go by. The walls on each side of the channel are worth a look as there are many caves to investigate. Schools of trevally, rainbow runners, surgeonfish and fusiliers gather in the channel in vast numbers, but you are also likely to see gropers, emperors and turtles. Don't forget to have a look at the sandy rubble as spider shells, helmet shells and even mantis shrimps shelter here.

OPPOSITE TOP: Two manta rays cruise about the aptly named Manta Ray Bommie.

OPPOSITE BOTTOM: Schools of painted sweetlips gather under the pontoon in Lady Musgrave Lagoon.

Lady Musgrave Lagoon is huge and dotted with countless coral heads in depths from 4m to 7m. While fun to dive during the day, especially around the Lady Musgrave Cruises Pontoon as it swarms with fish, the lagoon is at its best at night. After dark all manner of critters emerge from the sand and coral. A good torch will reveal hermit crabs, coral crabs, hingebeak shrimps, nudibranchs, flatworms, lionfish, scorpionfish, sleeping parrotfish and even the odd snake eel.

Some of the best diving at Lady Musgrave Island is found off its southern and eastern side, as here divers will find a drop-off in depths from 10m to 25m. Simply called **The Drop-Off**, you can jump in just about anywhere along the length of this wall and have a fantastic dive. This continuous wall is decorated with lovely gorgonians, soft corals, sea whips and black coral trees, plus home to a great range of reef fish. Larger sharks are seen here, like grey reef sharks and silvertip sharks, but whitetip reef sharks are also quite common. All the big stuff hangs out along this wall; pelagic fish, turtles, eagle rays, gropers and even olive sea snakes. But bring a torch with you, as caves undercut this wall and provide shelter for crayfish, tasselled wobbegongs, gropers, red emperors and swarms of baitfish. This part of the reef is rarely dived as it is exposed to the weather, but if you can get out here you will be justly rewarded with spectacular diving.

Lady Musgrave Island is a very under-rated dive destination, but it has a brilliant range of dive sites and is home to a wonderful array of marine life.

LADY MUSGRAVE ISLAND DIVE DATA

HOW TO GET THERE – A day boat departs from the town of Seventeen Seventy. The odd liveaboard boat also visits Lady Musgrave Island, usually departing from Bundaberg. Regional flights arrive daily at Bundaberg Airport.

BEST TIME TO VISIT – Year round the diving is great at Lady Musgrave Island, but manta rays are far more common over the winter months.

VISIBILITY – 15m to 30m on the outer reef, 10m to 15m in the lagoon.

CURRENTS – Mild currents are common around the island and often used to do drift dives, but strong currents are experienced around the lagoon channel.

WATER TEMPERTURE – Summer highs of 27°C to winter lows of 19°C.

OPPOSITE: Boer's batfish are found at many of the dive sites around Lady Musgrave Island.

WEIRD AND WONDERFUL REEF FISH

Over 1500 species of fish live on the Great Barrier Reef, and new species are being discovered every year. While the colourful and common reef fish are lovely to watch, there are some weird and wonderful reef fish you should keep an eye out for.

The lacy scorpionfish (*Rhinopias aphanes*) is such a well camouflaged fish that they are rarely seen by divers. This spectacular fish uses its camouflage to blend in with the corals so it can ambush other fish that swim too close to its mouth. Growing to a length of 23cm, consider yourself very lucky if you see a lacy scorpionfish.

A far more common scorpionfish seen on the Great Barrier Reef is the leaf scorpionfish (*Taenianotus triacanthus*). Rarely more than 10cm long, these pretty fish are seen in a kaleidoscope of colours – white, yellow, pink, red, brown and a mix of these. They usually sit amongst the corals and slowly rock side to side, just like a leaf.

A number of frogfish species inhabit reef waters, with the giant frogfish (*Antennarius commersonii*) and painted frogfish (*Antennarius pictus*) the species that divers are most likely to encounter. These strange fish walk on their fins and use a lure attached to their head to attract prey close enough so they can be grabbed.

Divers will need to spend a bit of time searching sand or coral rubble to see a Pegasus sea moth (*Eurypegasus draconis*) on the Great Barrier Reef. These incredible fish are amazing to watch as they weave across the bottom, and if you find a pair their mating dance is just magic.

A tiny species of seahorse is also found on the Great Barrier Reef, the Bargibant's pygmy seahorse (*Hippocampus bargibanti*). Not much bigger than a grain of rice these minute seahorses live on similarly patterned gorgonians. They appear to be a deep water species on the Great Barrier Reef, generally only found in depths greater than 30m, and are so small they can be extremely difficult to find.

Other weird and wonderful fish to look out for on the Great Barrier Reef are shrimpfish, ghost pipefish, velvetfish and snake eels.

OPPOSITE TOP: A rare species only occasionally seen on the Great Barrier Reef is the cryptic lacy scorpionfish.

OPPOSITE BOTTOM: More commonly seen in reef waters is the lovely leaf scorpionfish.

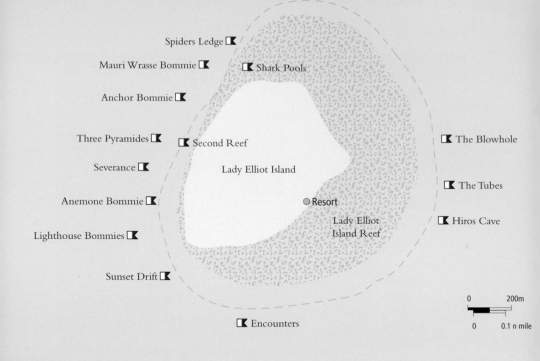

Spiders Ledge ◖◗

Mauri Wrasse Bommie ◖◗

Anchor Bommie ◖◗

◖◗ Shark Pools

Three Pyramides ◖◗   ◖◗ Second Reef

Severance ◖◗

Lady Elliot Island

Anemone Bommie ◖◗

◉ Resort

Lighthouse Bommies ◖◗

◖◗ The Blowhole

◖◗ The Tubes

◖◗ Hiros Cave

Lady Elliot
Island Reef

Sunset Drift ◖◗

0   200m

0   0.1 n mile

◖◗ Encounters

LADY ELLIOT ISLAND

There is a tiny coral cay located at the very southern tip of the Great Barrier Reef. This special island is the best place in Australia to see manta rays, but is also blessed with an abundance of other wonderful marine creatures. It is one of the jewels of the Great Barrier Reef and is called Lady Elliot Island.

Located 80km northeast of Bundaberg, Lady Elliot Island was discovered in 1816 by a ship bearing the same name. At the time this 45 hectare island was covered in thick forest and home to millions of nesting sea birds. That was until guano miners arrived in 1863. Over a ten year period the guano miners cut down almost every tree and stripped the island bare of its guano rich soil. During this time a lighthouse was built on the island, and once the miners left, the lighthouse keepers were the only ones that got to enjoy the island and its lovely coral reefs for the next one hundred years.

The island would probably still be an environmental disaster if not for Bundaberg businessman Don Adams who got permission to build an airstrip and start a tourism venture on Lady Elliot Island in 1969. Don also started an ambitious program of replanting trees, which worked incredibly well with much of the island now re-vegetated and the return of countless sea birds.

Today the resort on Lady Elliot Island is very eco-friendly, set amongst the trees and keeping its impact to a minimum. While some visitors come to the island to marvel at the sea birds, the great majority come to snorkel or dive its fringing coral reefs, which are some of the most spectacular on the entire Great Barrier Reef.

The most iconic dive site at Lady Elliot Island is a collection of small coral outcrops off the western side of the island known as **Lighthouse Bommies**. Spread across a sandy bottom in depths from 8m to 15m, these small bommies are decorated with lovely hard corals, soft corals and gorgonians and home to

OPPOSITE: Lady Elliot Island is famous for its wonderful manta rays.

213

numerous reef fish and invertebrates. But the main attraction at Lighthouse Bommies are manta rays, and they rarely disappoint.

Manta rays visit this group of bommies to get cleaned. It is common to see two or three manta rays hovering over the bommies while dozens of tiny cleaner wrasse go to work to remove parasites from their skin. Divers can generally get quite close to photograph and observe the manta rays if they stay low, but avoid chasing them as they will simply swim off.

Besides the manta rays Lighthouse Bommies is a great place to see tasselled wobbegong sharks. These flat body sharks like to shelter in the many ledges and caves that riddle the bommies, and being ambush predators they await prey to swim within striking range. Also common are whitetip reef sharks, leopard sharks, stingrays, spotted eagle rays and turtles.

The fish life seen around these bommies is amazing; Maori wrasse, barramundi cod, gropers, coral trout, snapper, sweetlips, surgeonfish and trevally. And if you are lucky the resident bottlenose dolphin may even make an appearance.

There are about twenty other dive sites found around Lady Elliot Island, and with currents quite common drift diving is popular. Another popular site on the western side of the island is **Anchor Bommie**. This tower of coral rises 12m above the sandy sea floor and is always buzzing with marine life. Riddled with ledges and caves, the bommie is often infested with schools of cardinalfish and baitfish, which in turn get feasted upon by trevally, coral trout and other predators. Parting this curtain of fish will often reveal tasselled wobbegongs, moray eels, octopus, crayfish and coral cod. Turtles and gropers are also common at Anchor Bommie, but some of its smaller residence are worth looking for – nudibranchs, cleaner shrimps and leaf scorpionfish.

Manta rays are often seen at Anchor Bommie, but the sand around the bottom is also worth a close look as stingrays, whitetip reef sharks and shovelnose rays rest here, and a huge colony of garden eels live in the sand in this area.

There are a number of other wonderful bommies off the western side of the island, at dive sites like **Maori Wrasse Bommie**, **Three Pyramids** and **Anemone Bommie**, all of which are brilliant to explore. Closer to shore on this side of the island is a long ridge of coral called **Second Reef**. This lovely reef is found in depths from 4m to 12m and is covered in pretty hard corals. Turtles are very common on this reef, but divers also see pretty reef fish and schools of surgeonfish, trevally and sweetlips.

Since the ship *Lady Elliot* first sighted the island in 1816 a number of vessels

OPPOSITE TOP: A diver descends into the Blowhole, one of the most spectacular dive sites at Lady Elliot Island.

OPPOSITE BOTTOM: Many schooling fish are seen at Lighthouse Bommies, including sawtail surgeonfish.

have come to grief on the island's fringing reef. Most of these have completely broken up, but one shipwreck remains in one piece, the *Severance*. This yacht sank in 1998 and now rests in 21m, and while compact it is a fun shipwreck to explore. Much of the boat, including its mast and rigging, remains in place but is now covered in lovely soft corals. A surprising number of fish reside on and around the wreck, including cobia, sweetlips, gropers, coral trout, trevally and emperors. But divers will also see stingrays, turtles and reef sharks at this site. Macro photographers will find a surprising variety of small subjects, including pipefish, cleaner shrimps, coral crabs, hermit crabs, scorpionfish and blennies.

The **Shark Pools** is dive site that is not often dived as it is shallow and much of the coral is dead, but it is a great place to see sharks. Only 3m to 8m deep, this site is a maze of caves and gutters, which are a perfect spot for whitetip reef sharks and tawny nurse sharks to rest. But this site is also a good place to see turtles, gropers and also blacktip reef sharks.

In deeper water beyond the Shark Pools is a series of ledges known as **Spiders Ledge**, where larger sharks are often sighted. In depths from 12m to 20m divers often see grey reef sharks, blacktip sharks and even the odd bull shark.

Drift diving is popular right around Lady Elliot Island, allowing divers to explore two or three dive sites at a time. Two of the more popular drift diving sites are **Sunset Drift** and **Encounters**, located off the southern end of the island. The coral gardens and bommies in this area are found in depths from 10m to 18m and this is a good spot to see gropers, barracuda, reef sharks, turtles and manta rays.

The eastern side of Lady Elliot Island is often affected by rough weather, so not always dived, but if conditions allow divers will find a pretty coral wall on this side of the island. This wall drops to 20m and is undercut with numerous caves. **The Tubes** and **Hiros Cave** are two lovely dive sites here, but the best is called **The Blowhole**.

Descending at The Blowhole divers see a large black hole in the reef top at 14m. This is the entrance to an L-shaped cave that exits on the reef wall at 22m. This tube like cave is large enough to drive a bus through, so can easily accommodate a boat load of divers. The cave is often filled with baitfish and glassfish that can form a curtain across the cave mouth. Mangrove jacks, coral trout, squirrelfish, pufferfish and sweetlips shelter in the cave alongside stingrays, turtles and the odd tasselled wobbegong shark.

OPPOSITE TOP: Divers will encounter many shark and ray species at Lady Elliot Island, such as the cowtail stingray.

OPPOSITE BOTTOM: The *Severance* wreck is a wonderful dive site as the yacht is mostly intact.

The walls each side of the cave are decorated with pretty gorgonians and soft corals, and home to numerous reef fish. But divers should keep an eye out to the blue as Spanish mackerel, barracuda, grey reef sharks, turtles, eagle rays, manta rays and silvertip sharks patrol this area.

Allow at least a week to discover all of the delightful dive sites at Lady Elliot Island, as many of the best sites you will want to dive again and again.

LADY ELLIOT ISLAND DIVE DATA

HOW TO GET THERE – The easiest way to dive Lady Elliot Island is to stay on the island at the wonderful resort. Flights to the island depart from Bundaberg and Hervey Bay, which are both serviced by regional airlines. The odd liveaboard boat also visits Lady Elliot Island at different times of the year.

BEST TIME TO VISIT – Year round the diving is excellent at Lady Elliot Island, but manta ray numbers increase over the winter months, and humpback whales are also common at this time of the year.

VISIBILITY – 20m to 30m.

CURRENTS – Mild currents are common around the island and often used to do drift dives.

WATER TEMPERTURE – Summer highs of 27°C to winter lows of 19°C.

ABOVE: Hinge-beak shrimps are often found sheltering in caves at Lady Elliot Island.

OPPOSITE: Anchor Bommie often gets swamped with schools of glassfish, which are in turn feasted upon by large coral trout.

– FEATURE –
MANTA MAGIC

Arriving at Lady Elliot Island by plane gives visitors a spectacular view of this magic island. But if you look closely you will dozens of black diamond shapes in the waters around the island, as Lady Elliot Island is one of the best places in the world to have a close encounter with manta rays. The manta rays seen around the island are the smaller of the two species, the reef manta ray (*Manta alfredi*), which still grow to an impressive 5.5m in width. Manta rays are encountered year round at Lady Elliot Island, but their numbers appear to increase over the winter months. Why these giant rays love this island is not really understood, but they aggregate at Lady Elliot Island to feed, get cleaned and possibly to mate.

A research project, called Project Manta, has been studying these manta rays for many years and using photo-identification of the distinctive belly markings they have recorded over 600 individual rays visiting the island. Further research may unlock some of the secret world of manta rays, but for now diving with these majestic creatures is one of the major highlights of a visit to Lady Elliot Island.

DIVE OPERATORS & RESORTS

The following is a list of dive operators and resorts within the Great Barrier Reef region.

LIZARD ISLAND

Lizard Island Resort – www.lizardisland.com.au
> One of the most luxurious and private resorts on the Great Barrier Reef. A dive centre is part of the resort complex, operating daily boat dives around the island and to the nearby Ribbon Reefs.

PORT DOUGLAS

ABC Scuba Diving – www.abcscubadivingportdouglas.com.au
> A dive charter operator that are geared for small groups.

Aroona – www.aroonaluxuryboatcharters.com.au
> Available for private liveaboard charters to the Ribbon Reefs and other destinations.

Blue Dive – www.bluedive.com.au
> Offer day tips and overnight liveaboard trips on the vessel MV *The Boss* to the local reefs off Port Douglas.

Calypso Reef Cruises – www.calypsoreefcruises.com
> Operate a day boat to the reefs off Port Douglas.

Eye to Eye Marine Encounters – www.marineencounters.com.au
> Offer special expeditions to see minke whales, sharks and other reef creatures.

Phoenix – www.biancacharters.com.au
> Liveaboard charter available for group bookings to explore the Ribbon Reefs, Northern Coral Sea Reefs and Far Northern Reefs.

Poseidon Cruises – www.poseidon-cruises.com.au
> Offer day trips for divers and snorkelers to the reefs off Port Douglas.

Quicksilver Cruises – www.quicksilver-cruises.com
 Provide day trips to explore the Agincourt Reefs off Port Douglas.
Silversonic – www.silverseries.com.au
 Offer day trips for divers and snorkelers to the reefs off Port Douglas.
Tech Dive Academy – www.tech-dive-academy.com
 Offer Tech diving courses and dive trips to the reefs of Port Douglas.

CAIRNS

Cairns Dive Centre – www.cairnsdive.com.au
 This dive centre offer day trips and short liveaboard trips to the local reefs off Cairns.
Compass Cruises – www.compasscruises.com.au
 Operate a day boat to the local reefs off Cairns.
Deep Sea Divers Den – www.diversden.com.au
 One of the oldest dive shops in Cairns they offer day trips and short liveaboard trips to the local reefs, and trips to the Ribbon Reefs on Taka.
Down Under Cruise and Dive – www.downunderdive.com.au
 Offer day trips to the local reefs on their vessel Osprey 5.
Great Adventures – www.greatadventures.com.au
 Operate day trips to Green Island and the outer reefs.
Ocean Freedom – www.oceanfreedom.com.au
 Day boat operation to the local reefs off Cairns.
Passions of Paradise – www.passions.com.au
 Day trips to the reefs off Cairns.
Pro Dive Cairns – www.prodivecairns.com
 One of the biggest dive shops in Cairns that offer three day liveaboard trips to the local reefs on their fleet of boats.
Reef Encounter – www.reefencounter.com.au
 Offer two to four day liveaboard dive trips to the local reefs off Cairns.
Reef Experience – www.reefexperience.com.au
 Charter boat running day trips to the local Cairn's reefs.
Reef Magic Cruises – www.reefmagiccruises.com
 Offer day trips to the reefs off Cairns.
Rum Runner – www.rumrunnercairns.com.au
 This liveaboard charter vessel runs two day trips to the local reefs off Cairns, but is available for longer trips to the Ribbon Reefs and Holmes Reef.
Seastar Cruises – www.seastarcruises.com.au
 Day trips to the reefs off Cairns.
Silverswift – www.silverseries.com.au

Offers day trips to the reef for snorkelers and divers.

Spirit of Freedom — www.spiritoffreedom.com.au
> One of Australia's premier liveaboard charter boats offering trips to the Ribbon Reefs, Osprey Reef and Far Northern Reefs.

Spoilsport (Mike Ball Dive Expeditions) — www.mikeball.com
> Spoilsport is one of the best liveaboard vessels in the world and operates charters to the Ribbon Reefs, Osprey Reef, Northern Coral Sea Reefs and Far Northern Reefs out of Cairns. But Spoilsport also does special expedition trips to the SS *Yongala* and to the wrecks of Torres Strait.

Sunlover Reef Cruises — www.sunlover.com.au
> Day trips to the local reefs off Cairns.

Taka — www.taka.com.au
> This liveaboard is available for trips to the Ribbon Reefs that vary in length from three to seven days.

Tusa Dive — www.tusadive.com
> A Cairns based dive shop that operate the day boat Tusa T6 to the reefs off Cairns.

MISSION BEACH

Mission Beach Dive — www.missionbeachdive.com
> Operate two charter boats offering day trips to the reef and Dunk Island.

TOWNSVILLE

Adrenaline Dive — www.adrenalindive.com.au
> Townsville based dive shop that offer day trips and liveaboard charters to the local reefs and SS *Yongala*.

Kalinda Charters — www.kalinda.com.au
> Liveaboard charter boat that offers group bookings to dive the reefs off Townsville and the SS *Yongala*. Also does special trips to the Far Northern Reefs each year.

Pleasure Divers — www.pleasuredivers.com.au
> Based on Magnetic Island Pleasure Divers organise dives around Magnetic Island, the local reefs and to the SS *Yongala*.

Remote Area Dive — www.remoteareadive.com.au
> Townsville based dive shop that offer dive trips to Pelorus and Orpheus Islands.

Yongala Dive — www.yongaladive.com.au
> Based at Alva Beach, Yongala dive operate daily dive trips to the wonderful SS *Yongala*.

WHITSUNDAYS

Atlantic Clipper – www.atlanticclipper.com.au
> This liveaboard offers a three day dive/sail trip around the Whitsunday Islands.

Cruise Whitsundays – www.cruisewhitsundays.com
> Operate Reefworld and Reefsleep, which are day trips to the reef or overnight accommodation on their reef pontoon.

Diving Whitsundays – www.divingwhitsundays.com
> Booking agents for a number of charter boats offering diving in the Whitsunday area.

Hamilton Island – www.hamiltonisland.com.au
> The biggest resort in the Whitsundays, there is a dive centre on the island that offers dive trips around the Whitsunday Islands or to the outer reef.

Illusions – www.illusion.net.au
> Operate day trips to the Whitsunday Islands that includes diving.

Islandive – www.islandive.com
> Booking agents for number of charter boats offering diving in the Whitsunday area.

Kiana Sail and Dive – www.mskiana.com
> Liveaboard vessel that offer three day dive/sail trips to the Whitsunday Islands and outer reef.

One and Only Hayman Island – www.hayman.oneandonlyresorts.com
> One of the most exclusive resorts in Australia, it also has a dive centre that offers dive trips around the Whitsunday Islands or to the outer reef.

Powerplay – www.powerplaycat.com
> Liveaboard offering three day dive/sail trips around the Whitsunday Islands.

Summertime – www.summertime-whitsundays.com
> This liveaboard offers a three day dive/sail trip around the Whitsunday Islands.

Whitsunday Dive Adventures – www.whitsundaydivecentre.com
> Offer day dive trips aboard MV *Mantaray* to the Whitsunday Islands from Airlie Beach.

Whitsunday Diving Academy – www.whitsundaydivingacademy.com.au
> Located near Airlie Beach this dive shop offers diver training and boat dives to the Whitsunday Islands.

KEPPEL ISLANDS

> Unfortunately no charter boats are operating in this area at the time of publication.

HERON ISLAND
Heron Island Resort – www.heronisland.com

Heron Island Resort is one of the oldest resorts on the Great Barrier Reef and has a dive centre that takes divers to the best dive sites around this lovely coral cay.

BUNDABERG, SEVENTEEN SEVENTY & YEPPOON
Adori Charters – www.capreefcruises.com.au

Liveaboard charter boat based in Yeppoon and available for group bookings to the Capricorn and Bunker Groups.

Big Cat Reality – www.bigcatreality.com

A liveaboard vessel based in Bundaberg that offers dive trips to the Capricorn and Bunker Groups, Lady Elliot Island, Swain Reefs and Southern Coral Sea Reefs.

Bundaberg Aqua Scuba – www.aquascuba.com.au

Bundaberg based dive shop that operate dive trips to Lady Musgrave Island.

Lady Musgrave Cruises – www.lmcruises.com.au

Based at Seventeen Seventy, Lady Musgrave Cruises operate day trips to Lady Musgrave Island for divers and snorkelers.

Professional Diving Services – www.professionaldiveservices.com.au

Brisbane based company that organise tours to dive the Capricorn and Bunker Groups, SS *Yongala* and other locations on the Great Barrier Reef.

LADY ELLIOT ISLAND
Lady Elliot Island Eco Resort – www.ladyelliot.com.au

Located on the beautiful Lady Elliot Island, this resort has a range of accommodation and a dive centre that will take divers to the best sites around this wonderful island at the end of the Great Barrier Reef.

TRAVEL INFORMATION

Most visitors to Australia have the Great Barrier Reef on the top of their list of places to visit, and with over two million visitors a year many of them fulfil that wish. The following travel information about Australia and the Great Barrier Reef will assist you to make your dream of visiting this coral wonderland a little easier.

TRANSPORT

With the Great Barrier Reef covering such a large area tourists have a wide choice of access points to journey to the reef. The main gateway city is Cairns, which has an international airport and is serviced by domestic flights from across Australia. Other gateway cities include Townsville, Airlie Beach, Gladstone and Bundaberg, all of which have domestic airports that connect with flights across Australia. However, international flights to and from Cairns Airport are very limited, so many overseas visitors may have to look into flying into Brisbane or Sydney and then transferring on a domestic flight.

Of course flying is not the only way to travel around Australia, but it is the quickest and cheapest generally. Bus and rail service the Queensland coastline, and these services will be required to visit some of the other access points to the reef like Port Douglas, Mission Beach and Yeppoon. A hire car is the other option, and will be required if you want to get to Alva Beach or Seventeen Seventy, as these towns are off the bus and rail network. The road network in Queensland is generally good, but the main coastal highway can be cut at times over the summer cyclone season due to flooding rains.

ENTRY REQUIREMENT

A valid passport is required to enter Australia, and all visitors (except New Zealanders) require a visa prior to arrival – visit www.border.gov.au for visa information.

MONEY

The Australia dollar is the only accepted currency in Australia. Most dive operators, resorts and hotels are happy to receive payment by credit card. Banks and ATMs are found throughout Queensland.

TIPPING

Tipping is not required or expected in Australia as everyone is paid a minimum wage.

POWER

The electricity in Australia is 240 volts AC 50Hz. Power points are three flat pins standard. Power point adaptors for overseas appliances are available in many hotels, resorts and on liveaboard dive boats, or can be purchased from airports or luggage shops.

LANGUAGE & CULTURE

English is the language that most Australian's speak, though some Aussie slang terms may be difficult for people from overseas to understand. Many dive guides and instructors employed on the Great Barrier Reef come from countries across the planet, so don't be surprised to find that your dive guide is English, Japanese or German.

Australian culture is hard to define, but is based around enjoying the outdoors and celebrating life, with Aussies loving to eat, drink and celebrate with just about anyone. Most Australians are very easy going and accepting of other cultures, as Australia is a multi-cultural society.

HEALTH

Australia is often viewed as a country overflowing with dangerous animals, but very few visitors ever come face to face with these creatures. Many snakes and spiders in Australia are highly venomous, but unless you go looking for them, and harass them, you are unlikely to ever encounter these critters. Sharks are found in reef waters, but most species encountered by divers and snorkelers are harmless and pose little threat to people.

Crocodiles are common in the tropical north of Australia, so rivers, creeks and waterholes are best avoided. Most of these are posted with warning signs, but if there is no sign use some common sense and don't go for a swim in the local creek, find a swimming pool instead. Also be aware that the inshore waters adjacent to the Great Barrier Reef are mainly murky with lots of mangrove areas where box-jellyfish are found. The stinger season is October to May, a time when it is best not to swim on coastal beaches adjacent to the reef. Fortunately box jellyfish are rarely seen on the Great Barrier Reef.

Although the top half of Australia is in a tropical zone there are few tropical diseases in the country that visitors need to worry about. Dengue Fever and Ross River Fever outbreaks occasional occur in Cairns and Townsville during the wet season, and as these are mosquito-borne diseases the best way to prevent them is to cover up at night and wear insect repellent.

One of the biggest risks to your health while on the Great Barrier Reef is sunburn, with Australia having very high UV readings, even on cloudy days. Be sun aware, wear a hat, sunglasses and sunscreen, and remember Australia has the highest incidents of skin cancer in the world. You can even get sunburnt while snorkelling, so cover up while in the water with a wetsuit or lycra suit, this will not only protect you from the sun but also from stinging jellyfish.

REFERENCES & FURTHER READING

Dangerous Sea Creatures by Neville Coleman, Underwater Geographic, 1999.

Discover Heron Island by Neville Coleman, Underwater Geographic, 1988.

Diving Australia by Neville Coleman and Nigel Marsh, Periplus Editions, 1997.

Great Barrier Reef by Isobel Bennett, Lansdowne Press, 1981.

Indo-Pacific Sea Fishes by Neville Coleman, Underwater Geographic, 2003.

Lady Elliot Island by Anthony Walsh, 2006

Reader's Digest Book of the Great Barrier Reef, Readers Digest, 1990.

Scuba Divers Guide Australia's Southern Great Barrier Reef by Tom Byron, Aqua Sports Publications, 1987.

Scuba Divers Guide Australia's Central Great Barrier Reef by Tom Byron, Aqua Sports Publications, 1987.

Scuba Divers Guide Cairns & Australia's Northern Great Barrier Reef by Tom Byron, Aqua Sports Publications, 1987.

Scuba Divers Guide Whitsunday Islands by Tom Byron, Aqua Sports Publications, 1987.

Sharks and Rays of Australia by Peter Last and John Stevens, CSIRO, 1994.

The Coral Battleground by Judith Wright, Thomas Nelson Australia, 1977.

The Dive Sites of the Great Barrier Reef and the Coral Sea by Neville Coleman and Nigel Marsh, New Holland Publishers, 1996.

UK £14.99